Sunset *Over* Java

For my family and friends born in the United States, and in memory of my mentor, William W. Laird

SUNSET
OVER JAVA

Jacobus E. de Vries

Jacobus E. de Vries
617 Fearrington Post
Pittsboro, NC 27312

Printed in the United States of America

ISBN-13: 978-1515037958

SUNSET OVER JAVA
Table of Contents

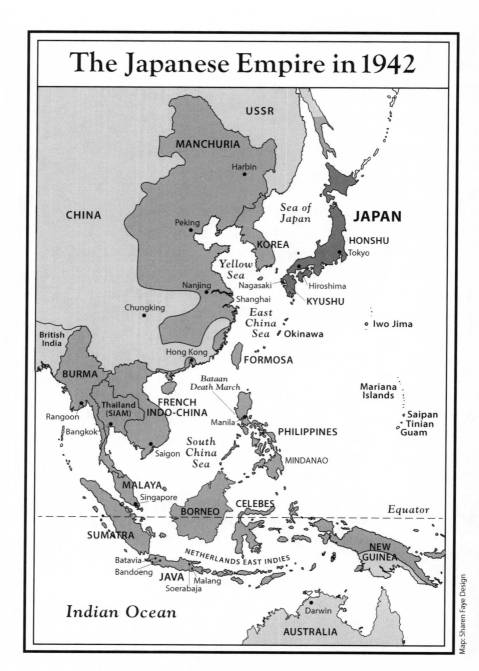

The Japanese Empire in 1942

USSR

MANCHURIA

Harbin

CHINA

Peking

Sea of Japan

JAPAN

KOREA

HONSHU

Tokyo

Yellow Sea

Nanjing

Nagasaki

Hiroshima

Shanghai

KYUSHU

Chungking

East China Sea

Okinawa

Iwo Jima

British India

Hong Kong

FORMOSA

Mariana Islands

BURMA

Bataan Death March

Rangoon

Thailand (SIAM)

FRENCH INDO-CHINA

Manila

PHILIPPINES

Saipan
Tinian
Guam

Bangkok

South China Sea

Saigon

MINDANAO

MALAYA

Singapore

CELEBES

Equator

BORNEO

SUMATRA

NEW GUINEA

NETHERLANDS EAST INDIES

Batavia

Bandoeng

JAVA

Malang

Soerabaja

Indian Ocean

Darwin

AUSTRALIA

Map: Sharen Faye Design

As they battled to free the Philippines, the Americans avoided Java, Sumatra and Borneo to their south. That strategy shortened the war.

A Note to the Reader

When the Japanese Imperial Navy attacked the American Navy at Pearl Harbor in 1941, I had no idea that the coming years would tragically change the lives of everyone in my family. Not all of us would survive. My parents had grown up in the Netherlands and had moved to the Netherlands East Indies in the 1920's. I was the youngest of their four children and was born in Batavia on the island of Java in 1934, in what is now Jakarta, Indonesia.

My purpose in writing this memoir is to illustrate for my American family and friends a part of the Pacific War that is not well known, mostly because few Americans fought in our region. Most accounts have focused on the heroism and terrible sacrifices in American lives as the men in the US Navy, Marines, Army and Air Force fought their way toward Tokyo. As they battled to free the Philippines, the Americans avoided Java, Sumatra and Borneo to their south. That strategy shortened the war. But it had frightful, unintended consequences for those of us in the Japanese prison camps who prayed for our liberation.

A second reason for writing this personal story is to illustrate for younger readers how resilient we can be. That is the positive part of my story. Even when our lives are turned upside down and pulled apart by forces beyond our control we learn we can survive some major shocks. With help from family and friends, and even total strangers, people can rebuild their lives. In my case, that included a turnaround once I was on my own in the US Army, followed by a Harvard education and a successful career.

Jacobus E. (Jack) de Vries
Fearrington Village, NC

Chapter One

THUNDERCLAPS

"You are free to go," he said. That makes no sense. We know we can't leave. There are no signs that anything has changed. It is all still the same. I'm stunned and don't know what to think. But now, all around me, the older boys are yelling to each other and I find a grown-up and ask him.

"Did he say we are free to go?"

"Yes, it's true—the war is over — we can all go home!"

I don't understand it, but now I feel wild excitement too. My home is much too far away and I can't go there by myself because I have no family here. They are all in other prison camps. Still, this is what we have all been hoping for and dreaming about. That magic land of After-the-War, was it really coming now? This is not how I thought it would come. There have been no sounds of war, no artillery. No American planes overhead. All of a sudden? And just an announcement?

I am ten years old, a Dutch boy in a Japanese prison camp in the Dutch East Indies. We live on the island of Java, in what is now Indonesia. It is August 1945, and I am sitting at a long table with other boys, cutting vegetables in the central kitchen. Someone yells that we have to stop and come to the big field right away. It is late afternoon and we line up military-style as usual. The Japanese camp commander gives a very short speech in Malay, and one of the Dutch grown-ups translates for us:

"To relieve the suffering of his brave and loyal subjects, His Celestial Majesty the Emperor of Japan has decided to end the war. We will maintain order until the Allies arrive. We will try to bring more food to the camp. The war is over. You are free to go."

I'm in a daze. We are all milling around, talking at once and getting crazy with excitement. Then someone yells: "Let's see if the gate is open!" So I run there with some of my friends. And there are the Japanese guards, with long gleaming bayonets on their rifles. They just stand there and the gate is wide open. There is no one outside that we can see, but we don't dare to step out. We are all deathly afraid to go near the tall barbed wire fence around the camp.

Did he say *the Emperor has decided to end the war*? Why? Did they just give up? I guess someone will explain later.

News from the Outside World

By the guardhouse, I see a big radio on a table outside, and men who are straining to hear all they can. News from the outside world! The men tell me that Radio Melbourne has said the war in Europe is over. Queen Wilhelmina has returned to Holland. They say there are reports of a powerfully devastating bomb that forced Nippon to surrender to the Americans.

That white Japanese flag with its red central "sun" has disappeared. We had all been ordered to bow to that flag as the symbol of the divine Emperor Hirohito. The sight of it meant immediate anxiety, and we hated it.

Figure 1 Japanese forces attacking Singapore in February 1942, flying both their national flag and the Rising Sun battle flag of the Japanese Navy. National Archives.

Now somebody has brought out a large Dutch flag— red, white and blue. That forbidden flag is right there, out in the open! I choke up. One wild surprise piled on another. My confusion melts into relief and excitement—anxious excitement. What does it mean? In this prison camp of young boys and older men there is no adult I can turn to for help or advice.

3

Soon all hell breaks loose, as the older boys in the barracks take shirts, shorts, any kind of clothing, and climb to the top of the woven bamboo wall surrounding the camp to trade clothing for food with the Indonesian natives outside. Once I smell and see this food, I ask one of the bigger boys to help me get some too. He takes one of my old shirts and climbs up to the top of the barbed wire and woven-bamboo wall. As he reaches down with my shirt, the native on the other side snatches it and runs. No food for me.

That night the excited commotion continues and I hear a rumor that a shed filled with mattresses of those who have died has been broken open. I go there, and in the pitch black, rummage around in a pile of kapok stuffing and find a piece of cloth. This time I trade it myself, through a hole in the woven bamboo wall, and get some rice wrapped in banana leaves. There is moonlight and I can find my way back to the barracks.

The next morning, my three friends and I sit cross-legged on our mattress and talk about our peace-time homes and about our parents and get ourselves all wound up with anticipation of a return to that world we only vaguely remember.

My home is very far away. It took us a day and a night to get here by train from West Java. I came here to Central Java with my mother and sister last November. Just six months ago I was separated from them and sent to this camp, 8 kilometers away, with a truckload of other boys.

When we arrived here in Kamp 7 in January of 1945, my small group of boys from Kamp 10 had been assigned some floor space in this old, condemned, Dutch Army base. We were anxious and confused at first because there was no adult in charge. We had come from a camp that had no adult male prisoners, only women and children. I learned later that there were about 5,000 older men here and about 800 young boys.

At first we were assigned to a small building near the gate. That was good because we could put our mattresses on the tile floor and there was no bunk above us. My nickname was "**Ko**" in those years, an abbreviation of Ja**co**bus, and later changed to Jack. For my American readers, I have also changed the first names of my siblings from the Dutch to "Jan, Bert and Joan."

Niels van Dijk, the boy sleeping on the next mattress made a pencil sketch of our sleeping area in "Amberawa Kamp 7" and it is included here (Fig. 2). My camping bed-roll, pillow and leather briefcase are at the right-hand side, labeled "K. de Vries."

Within about a week or two after we settled in at Kamp 7, we heard a loud roaring overhead. We raced outdoors to gape at a low-flying airplane coming right over our buildings. It was gone in a flash, but not so fast that we didn't see the huge Dutch red, white and blue colors on the plane's tail. We yelled with excited surprise and pointed toward the disappearing plane.

"Did you see that plane? What do those papers say? Oh, let me see, let me see......."

5

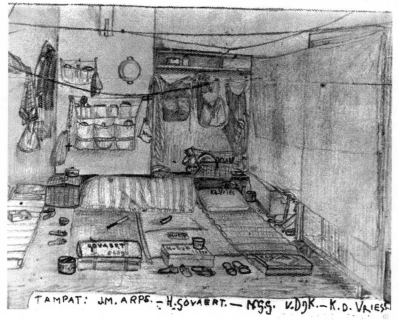

Figure 2 Sketch of my place in Ambarawa Kamp 7, 1945, Central Java. Drawn by Niels van Dijk. My "suitcase" was my father's old briefcase. Instead of toilet paper we used small cans of water, as shown in the foreground. The original title in Dutch was: "Our place is about three meters wide, because there was enough room for us four."

They were leaflets, in Dutch, telling us to keep our spirits up. Was this the beginning of the fighting that would bring the end of the war? Where did that plane come from? Our excited hopes reached a peak, but didn't last for long. Almost immediately, the guards were ordering us to collect every leaflet and hand them in at the guardhouse by the gate. The older men said to do what we were told, and so we did. And then—nothing. No more planes overhead. No news of any kind. Another disappointment, like all the false rumors we had heard so often, about the war being over "very soon." So we went back to just living from day to day, like dazed animals, thinking only about food.

Four Kids per Bed Sideways

A few months later, all 800 boys are moved into one large central barracks. This is much, much worse, because we are told to sleep four to a bed, sideways. This old military hospital barracks becomes extremely overcrowded. We are madly concentrated because the old wooden beds are stacked three high (Fig. 3). We have just enough space to lie down, shoulder to shoulder.

Figure 3 In Ambarawa Kamp 7, we later slept in stacked bunks, four per bunk bed, sideways. Drawing by D. H. Volz.

This was not an extermination camp, but it became a concentrated starvation camp, especially for the older, sickened men. Initially we had been interned in the city of Bandoeng (Bandung), where we had lived in houses with furniture and had enough to eat. Now we are imprisoned, jammed together and under Japanese Army control.

Hans, Niels, Jan and I share a mattress on one of these wooden hospital beds. They have many slats and joints and are crawling with lice. They look like deer ticks and are called *wandluizen*—bed bugs. They bite and begin to crawl on your legs and up your sides as soon as the lights go out. Blood comes out when you squeeze them. They leave blood streaks on the inside of your sweaty shirt collar.

Obsessed with Food

We are boys of 10, 11 or 12, and we are hungry. We talk about food all the time. I tell my bunkmates that in my house in Batavia before the war, there was usually a bowl of fruit on the sideboard in the dining room, and we just ignored it.

"Can you believe it, my brothers and sister and I would walk right by without taking anything? And when we didn't finish everything on our plate it was just thrown away. After the war we will never waste food again. Everybody agrees on that now. After the war we can linger over delicious food again."

Here in the camp, we try to eat as slowly as possible, to make that small rice portion last as long as we can. I eat with a demitasse spoon. It has a long stem and was probably used in our house to stir tall drinks before the war. In the morning we get a portion of tapioca jelly that looks and tastes like wallpaper paste. It isn't really food, but it is something in your stomach. We've seen that a bowl of this jelly turns to nothing but water overnight. For the middle of the day, we get a small square of un-leavened bread, which we carve carefully into smaller pieces to make it last as long as possible. In the evening we get a bowl of white rice and a cup of soup. Usually it has some sweet potato, cabbage, sweet potato leaves and other vegetables in it. The soup used to have some bits of meat in it, but now the camp only gets some animal intestines from time to time. Every

9

now and then we get a small ration of sugar. I keep my sugar in a small can and try to make it last as long as I can.

We ask each other where we think our families might be. Our fathers have long since been sent to separate camps, and I tell them my older brothers are probably still in Bandoeng in West Java, where I had last seen them. We hope that our mothers and sisters are still nearby in Kamp 10. That is where all of us young kids had come from in January. This new day, we are too confused to even imagine getting back there on our own.

We have only some shirts and shorts and no money. We've been sealed off from the outside world, with no way to get in touch with anybody. The possession of any radio was long since forbidden and punished by beheading. The stories of such executions had traveled fast throughout the camps. We'll just wait for the adults to tell us what to do.

Waiting for the Adults

The next morning another boy comes walking through the barracks, calling my name.

"Jack de Vries! (de Vries rhymes with "niece") Jack de Vries!"

"Yes, over here. What is it?"

"In Barracks Five, Mr. van der Ploeg wants to see you. Here is his name."

I take the little piece of paper and feel full of hope and excitement. All these good things are happening so quickly.

Figure 4 These were some of the boys in my overcrowded barracks in Ambarawa Kamp 7, still waiting to be reunited with their families. Photo taken by Lady Mountbatten's camera crew after our liberation.

It is a beautiful, sunny day and I practically skip across the grounds to the barracks with the sad old men.

These are the grown-ups who have been dying. So many of them have died. Their bodies are thin except for their feet and legs, which are swollen from wet beri-beri.

In later years I learned that beri-beri is caused by acute vitamin deficiency, and that liquid forms under the skin of the feet and legs, moves up to the rest of the body and eventually reaches the heart.

Wet beri-beri, dysentery and tuberculosis are killing more and more of the old men. Most of them can't work in the gardens anymore and they just shuffle around the camp. I wonder what it is like to starve and just not wake up. The beri-beri looks painful. Perhaps pain has stopped too.

The Japanese rules are for everyone who sees coffins being carried to the gate to stop what they are doing immediately and to bow—in respect for the dead. Those flimsy coffins are made of woven bamboo now. There is a blackboard near the gate where the names of the men who died the previous day are written in chalk. Half of these men perished during the last six months of Japanese rule. The end of the war came too late for a great many.

Only a few boys have died from disease—most of us just get weaker and thinner. I have fevers at night, and painful boils. Like other kids, I get mumps for the second time. We had been told that you couldn't get mumps again, but we did anyway. We all have attacks of diarrhea from time to time, and some suffer from amoebic dysentery. There is no toilet paper and very little soap, so the primitive hygiene of the open latrines means we are constantly re-infected. Diarrhea weakens you quickly.

I don't remember whether Kamp 7 had a hospital, but we knew there were no medicines in our camps anymore. If there was a "hospital" it was just a quiet place to die.

But now the war is over and they say we are going home! I'm excited and full of hope, and I expect more and more good news. I find Barracks Five and ask for Mr. van der Ploeg. A stranger steps forward and asks if I'm Jack de Vries.

"Yes, I am," I reply a bit shyly.

"Oh, I'm a friend of your father," he says. He seems kind.

"Let's go sit outside. After the camp commander's announcement yesterday, I walked out of the gate and hitch-hiked to Kamp 10," he says. "Oh yes, that's where my mother and sister are. I want to go there too!"

I'm smiling and my heart is pounding. But this kind stranger seems sad. He says he found his wife and daughter in Kamp 10; they are still alive but very, very weak, he says.

"Your dad and I worked in the same Ministry of Economic Affairs before the war, and my wife knew your mother too. Yesterday she told me that your Mom passed away three months ago. I'm so sorry to have to tell you this."

My happy feelings are gone in an instant. There is a sudden weight in the pit of my stomach. I catch my breath. "Passed away? No, no, that's a mistake! She is still there, I know it!"

It has never occurred to me that my mother would not once again be the center of my world when we were freed and when we all went home. Now this kind stranger tells me that he has just been to my mother's camp and that she died in May.

She is the Center of My World

But that can't be true! She is waiting for me—she has to be!
She is the center of my world and she cannot be gone. She
was there only seven months ago! I begin to cry and cry
and I cannot stop. Through my sobs, I hear this man say
"Jack, you can come with me. I'm going back to Kamp 10
to stay. My wife and daughter need me. Go get your things
and come back here right away—go!"

My suitcase is small. It was my father's old leather
briefcase. Inside, I have my children's Bible, a small photo
album, a toy black and white dairy cow, a little carved
wooden fish from Ceylon and a few clothes. No shoes. We
are all barefoot by now and we all sleep in our clothes.

My excited joy this morning has now become a dull
ache. In a daze, I get my little suitcase and walk out the
gate with this friend of my father's. We walk and walk,
down the dirt road from the garrison town of Ambarawa to
Kamp 10, the old walled prison out in the countryside,
about 8 kilometers from town.

We walk this dusty country road, and by late afternoon
we reach a little house on the right-hand side. It is
surrounded by rice paddies. Mr. van der Ploeg says that he
knows the Indonesian family here because this had been an
agricultural experimental station before the war.

"It's all right, Jack. I know them, and we can stop here
to sleep." The native woman gives me an enormous plate of
rice with a piece of salted fried fish, all for me. That night I
sleep in a real bed.

In the morning it is wondrously quiet. Is that the sound of chickens scratching outside? As I awake, my emotions well up again: excitement and dread at the same time. I can't believe my Mom is not going to be there to reassure me that all will be well again. My insides are a sickening mixture of relief and hope for a return to normal life and fierce denial about Mom's death. I don't know what to expect anymore and move in a daze.

It is another sunny morning. Now that I am out of the camp, I can see long distances again. Inside Kamp 7, I had worked in the sweet potato gardens, weeding with an old table knife. At a special spot in those gardens, you could see over the woven bamboo wall. You could glimpse the top of the Merapi volcano far away, out there in the outside world. Sometimes it had a small puff of smoke coming out. Now I am in that outside world, and I can see that volcano and the real horizon again.

The man and I walk the rest of the way toward my sister's camp. We are both barefoot, but the stones in the road no longer hurt our calloused feet. We are both skin-over-bones, with dark tans, and he is wearing worn-out shorts, too. When we walk into Banjoe Biroe (bahn you beeru) Kamp 10 through its huge gate, I remember that seven months ago this is where I last saw my mother and sister.

Our Mothers Didn't Know

In January, the Japanese had ordered that all boys ten or older had to pack their belongings and leave. Were we dangerous young men now, in Japanese eyes? Were we going to a men's camp? Was the food there better or worse?

Our mothers didn't know. All I knew was that my mother was very upset and tried not to show it. She gave me a roll-up camp mattress and packed my father's old briefcase with my last remaining things. When it came time to climb onto the trucks, we hugged one last time and tried hard to stop the tears. The last time I saw Mom and my older sister Joan was when they stood in a row of other women and girls near the gate and waved.

As the trucks began to move onto this same dirt road to Ambarawa, the older teenage boys yelled at us to stop crying and sing as hard as we could. We all stood in the open truck, with the wind on our faces getting stronger as we picked up speed. We sang into the wind, some short and easily-remembered tunes, with new Dutch words that defied the Japs. "Het zonnetje gaat van on scheiden, en Jappen bloed kleurt reeds het veld....." (The sun of Japan is setting and colors the fields red with their blood...) So we felt brave and "flink"—that great Dutch word for grown up and tough. Now it is seven months later, somehow the war is over, and I am coming back to find my sister.

"Joan, is it true? Is Mom not here anymore?"
She shakes her head.

"How did it happen?"

"I don't know. Mom was very thin and tired and then she went into the hospital and I was allowed to visit her. I thought she would get better and come back." Her voice trails off, and she bursts into tears. "I don't understand it Jack. Nobody told me Mom was going to die!"

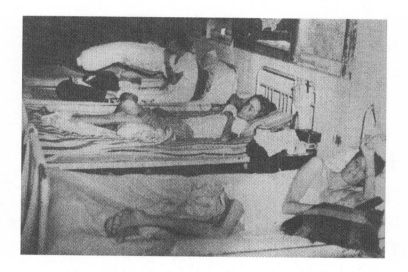

Figure 5 Starvation and disease nearly killed these women in Banjoe Biroe Kamp 10.

There are no photos of the camps during the Japanese occupation. This photo was taken by Lady Mountbatten's advance party right after we were freed in September 1945.

Joan is only twelve, very thin and bewildered. Together we return to the crowded stable and her sleeping area. Now I see Mom's suitcase and the empty place where she had slept. It begins to sink in that I will never see her again. I can't accept that and try hard to remember her face and her voice. I can't help the burning tears.

We don't know what to do. They say the war is over, but we are even more miserable now. Everything is upside down.

Are the two of us all that is left of our family? Is Dad still alive? Is he looking for us? And what about our older brothers, Jan and Bert? Are they still in Bandoeng where we last saw them? Of course Joan and I have no money and can't go anywhere. For now, we'll just wait and try to get more food. How did we get to this awful place to begin with? What are we doing here in a Japanese concentration camp in central Java, without the rest of our family?

Chapter Two

CHINA WAS THE PRIZE

Before the Japanese occupation, our lives on Java had been perfectly normal. I remembered it as quite happy, surrounded by my family and never being hungry or afraid. I was born on this island and had begun second grade when the war broke out.

As a little boy, I didn't understand why Japan was threatening to invade us in the Netherlands East Indies. Later on I learned that the Japanese had attacked the United States not because they thought they could conquer it, but to neutralize the US Navy while they conquered the oil fields of the Netherlands East Indies.

In his book *Pacific Onslaught*, Paul Kennedy summarizes concisely why the Japanese attacked the Western Allies in 1941:

"When Japan went to war with China in 1937, her armies by their very success moved further and further away from the homeland, needing more and more trucks to move the men, more armoured vehicles to protect thin-skinned transport, and more air cover to protect them all. And much more oil to fuel everything.

"Then came 1940 and a sudden curtailing of essential supplies; in September America imposed an oil embargo against 'all aggressors'—letting Japan know quite clearly that this was a category in which she herself was included.

"Almost ninety percent of Japan's oil supplies vanished at a stroke, together with important proportions of other essentials. Japan was faced with either abandoning the recently conquered territories, together with the loss of prestige and face no Eastern nation could afford, or else acquiring other sources of supply. As it happened, other sources of the essential oil were not far away: Borneo, Java and Sumatra could supply Japan's foreseeable needs...."

Our Oil Was Essential

Kennedy continues: "Japan obtained the sources of oil and the equally essential clear passageway for the oil to the mainland, in an explosion of military energy which astounded the world. The Japanese onslaught in the Far East was one of the most successful, swift and extensive campaigns in the history of warfare. Within four months they had captured Hong Kong, Malaya, Singapore, the Dutch East Indies, southern Burma and most of the Philippines; within another month Corregidor was to surrender and the British pushed out of Burma."

The extensive literature on these military developments may be condensed as follows:

In order to conquer the oil fields of the Dutch East Indies and safeguard the tanker routes from the Indies to their homeland, the Japanese had to eliminate the three major bastions of Allied strength that could destroy their "Southern Strategy." They knew they would have to knock out the American fleet in Hawaii, the British fleet at Singapore and the American Army Air Force in the Philippines.

They did so in four days.

The Empire of the Sun

Because they had already conquered Korea, Manchuria, Formosa and a major part of northern China in four years of war, the Japanese had developed superior military equipment as well as battle-hardened troops by the time they launched their attack on Pearl Harbor in December of 1941. The Zero fighter plane and the Long Lance naval torpedo were not matched by the Americans until some years later. On land, on the sea, and in the air, the Japanese military had trained men and machines in superior numbers and superior war-making abilities.

For example, while the Japanese Navy had six modern aircraft carriers, the only Allied carriers in the entire Pacific Basin were four US Navy carriers, far away in Hawaii. The British battleships defending Singapore were torpedoed by Japanese aircraft in the same way the American battleships at Pearl Harbor had been destroyed. Because Britain was desperately fighting the German Army in North Africa there was not a single British tank available to defend Malaya and Singapore.

In an astonishing disaster, General MacArthur failed to order the American Army Air Force bombers and fighters into the air as a Japanese air armada approached Manila a day after Pearl Harbor had been attacked. This critically important fighting force was destroyed on the ground at Clark Field.

Lastly, to complete the prescription for disaster, the Americans, British, Australians and Dutch were unanimous in their contempt for Japan as a primitive nation—as the makers of cheap toys. Everyone firmly believed that the Japanese could not build weapons of superior quality.

For Japan, it was all about colonizing China to obtain its vast resources. After they invaded China in 1937, the Japanese had fought with fanatical loyalty to their divine Emperor. They conquered a vast portion of Asia, stretching from Guadalcanal to Burma and from the frozen lands of Manchuria to the jungles of Java.

Japan's Shinto religion held Emperor Hirohito to be the divine descendant of the mystical sun goddess Amaterasu. As a result, the Japanese called their country "Dai Nippon," the Land of the Rising Sun. Their national flag showed the central sun: a red ball on a white field. Their naval battle flag is still in use today and is called the Rising Sun flag, filled with the red rays of the rising sun. Theirs was the "Empire of the Sun."

The Japanese Empire in 1942

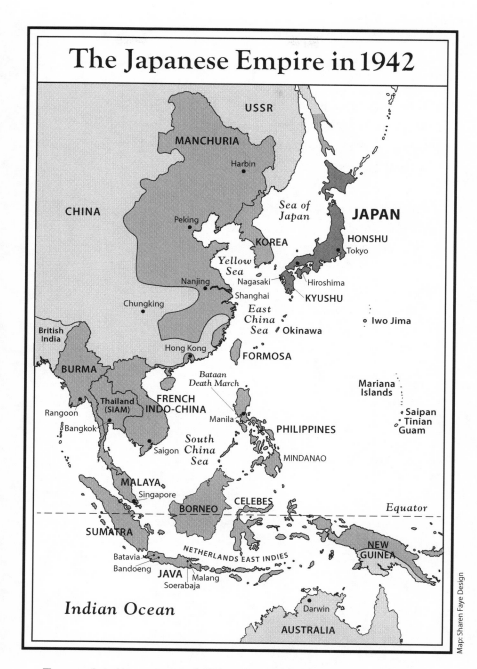

**To complete its conquest of China, Japan had to have its own source
of oil and a safe tanker route to its homelands.
In Burma, it had to stop Allied supplies from reaching China.**

Sunset Over Java

And so it was that my family, living on Java in 1941, was in the wrong place at the wrong time. We had no inkling of what the coming years of Japanese occupation might mean for us. Our parents tried to be reassuring, but of course they were guessing just like everyone else. It has been said that it is better not to know ahead of time how bad things will become in the future.

(A Timeline of Major Events is included on pages 157 to 159.)

Chapter Three

THE SPICE ISLANDS

My parents were born in the Netherlands, where Dad had finished his university education as an economist and Mom was a school teacher. In 1924, they had shipped out to the Netherlands East Indies, where he became a Government economist. As a Dutch colony since the seventeenth century, the East Indies attracted young people in Holland the way that California attracted young people in the Eastern United States. It was the land of opportunity, where people could have better career options, big houses, spacious grounds and a number of native servants. So my oldest brother, my sister and I were all born and raised on the island of Java. My second oldest brother, Bert, had been born in Holland when the family was on furlough.

As the Germans conquered the European continent and the Japanese attacked Pearl Harbor, we lived in Batavia, the capital city of the Netherlands East Indies, now called Jakarta, Indonesia.

Throughout this book I use names such as the Netherlands and Holland interchangeably with Nederland. Similarly the East Indies were synonymous with the Netherlands East Indies or the Dutch East Indies, and then renamed Indonesia after the war. Our capital city of Batavia was renamed Jakarta by the Indonesians after the war.

I have also used the word "Japs" because that is the word everyone used at that time, and this is a personal memoir.

A Good Life in Batavia

Our house at number 20 New Tamarind Lane was large, with brick walls that were white-washed. The roof was made of reddish-brown tile and the interior floors were also tiled. Like all the other houses in this tropical climate, our house was all on one floor. The roof was peaked to shed the monsoon rains. We had a large front yard with a half-moon gravel driveway and a spacious back yard with shade and fruit trees.

Figure 6 A typical Javanese landscape, with fertile rice paddies stretching to the foot of a volcano.

In addition to our educated Christian nanny, we had five servants, including the "djongos" (butler), the cook, the wash maid, the gardener and the chauffeur. We were lovingly cared for by our Dutch Eurasian nanny, "Juffie" (Missy), who spoke perfect Dutch, while the others spoke their native Sundanese.

We had a four-door American car, a navy blue La Salle, which we all loved. Our ice box had recently been replaced with a Frigidaire. On Sundays, we sometimes got a glass of cold Coca Cola at tea time on the veranda.

We had a good life. Batavia was the capital of the East Indies and was located on the northern shore of the island, right on the Java Sea and just south of the equator. The only seasons were the wet and the dry; it was always hot and often humid. Like all of the other Dutch houses, ours had no glass in the windows because we wanted the air circulation. (Air conditioning had not been invented yet.) There was no front door either. You simply stood on someone's veranda and called out "Spah'daah" which is Malay for "Hello, anybody home?"

We all slept under mosquito netting. Once you were in bed, the mosquito net was tucked in at the edge of the mattress. As a little boy, I remember standing up in bed and running my fingertips quickly down the grooves created by the taut net. It almost felt as if you were burning your fingertips, but my sister across the room and I would keep doing it anyway.

Furlough to Holland

My earliest childhood memories are about my family's furlough to Holland in 1938 when I was four. It was customary that Dutch civil servants, and most corporate employees, were rewarded with one month in Holland for every year of tropical service. We traveled by ship, of course, and it took about four weeks: Batavia to Rotterdam, via Ceylon and the Suez Canal. At that time, this was the biggest adventure of my life. Accompanied by Juffie, we enjoyed six months in Europe. My parents rented houses in Zoutelande for the summer and in Bilthoven where I had my fourth birthday in the fall. That winter I experienced my first frost and snow—quite exciting.

Figure 7 My mother teaching me to write. Holland, 1938.

When it came time to return to Java, we all visited my great-uncle and his family outside Geneva, Switzerland. I was his name-sake and we called him "Oom Ko" (ohm koh). His name was Jacobus E. de Vries, with the emphasis on the second syllable, and he had spent most of his life in the Dutch merchant marine in the Far East, before retiring to Switzerland with his French wife. He was a colorful figure full of adventure stories about the head hunters of Borneo and their weapons. I was full of admiration for his tiger skins, native daggers, arrows and shields.

Our Life Before the War

In Batavia, Dad worked downtown at the offices of the Ministry of Economic Affairs. I learned only much later that he was one of only two economists with a Ph.D. in the entire country. Doctorate degrees were few and far between in the 1930's, even in Holland. Before oil was discovered, the economy of the Dutch East Indies was based almost entirely on tropical plantation agriculture, and that was my father's specialty. Our tropical islands, with their rich volcanic soil, had become major exporters of sugar, rice, rubber, coffee, tea, tobacco and quinine.

Before Holland was occupied by the Germans in 1940, students from the Dutch East Indies had been educated in tropical agriculture in Wageningen, where Dad earned his degrees. Once it became impossible to travel to Europe, the head of the Ministry, Dr. van Mook (vahn moke), asked

Dad to create an agricultural faculty so that future generations could prepare for their careers on Java. As a result, in 1941, professor de Vries became the Dean of a new School of Tropical Agriculture at the University of Batavia, while continuing part-time at the Ministry of Economic Affairs.

Before the Japanese invasion, the four de Vries kids all went to school early in the mornings when it was coolest. After school, when I was in first grade, I would be taken to a nearby swimming pool where I earned my "Zwem Diploma"—but I dreaded having to jump from the high platform. When I hesitated too long, the swim teacher would climb up the ladder and jump off with her arms around me, imprisoning me. I hated that and still remember the air bubbles rushing past my face and into my nose. As it turned out, I grew to love swimming in later life.

The other very clear memory that has remained all these years is being taken to the large zoo, not far from our house. I was very interested in the huge elephants, the large *orang utan*, the shimmering peacocks and the large cement enclosure for the man-eating Komodo dragons, the largest lizards in the world.

After lunch, my sister and I were always told to take a nap. Too often we couldn't sleep and I still remember lying in bed and listening to the gardener raking leaves with a scratchy straw hand broom. That meant it was almost 4 o'clock and we would be allowed up again.

When we went on vacation, we would take a train or drive up into the mountains of West Java where it was much cooler. At other times, we went to the beach where, of course, we all got terrible sunburns. (Sunscreen lotions had not yet been invented and we were unaware of any risks of skin cancer.) My mother put Pond's Facial Cream on my shoulders; it had a distinctive fragrance that I still remember. That facial cream probably just helped fry my skin even more. I still remember how painful my shoulders were as the skin peeled off later. To each other, we would say "Don't touch, don't touch."

Figure 8 After a ride in Uncle Lo's convertible, 1937. From left to right: Mom, her younger brother Lo Berg, Bert, Jan, Joan, Jack and Juffie.

Often we were joined by my mother's blue-eyed younger brother, Uncle Lodewijk Berg (ohm loh). He was a handsome, dare-devil athlete, gym teacher and soccer coach. He was always full of confidence and would say he could do anything he really wanted to do. We would jump for joy when he swung into our driveway in his new Ford convertible with a hearty 'Hello, Hello!'

After the war, we learned that even he had starved to death in his prison camp. He was only 44 years old and died a month before the Japanese surrendered.

Storm Warnings

At the time of my seventh birthday, in October of 1941, we received three family members who were evacuated from Japan by the Dutch government's Foreign Service: our aunt Rins de Voogd and her two sons, Jan and Bert. The Dutch government feared an outbreak of war because the Netherlands, allied with the United States and Britain, had joined the oil embargo against Japan. Our government had stopped selling oil to the Japanese.

That October, Bert de Voogd and I shared the same birthday in Batavia. After a few weeks, my aunt and her sons boarded a ship for Canada. Our uncle Nico de Voogd remained at the Dutch consulate in Kobe, Japan. Once war did break out, Uncle Nico, along with other diplomats, was exchanged for Japanese diplomats interned in Allied nations. The exchange took place in the nearest neutral territory, which by then was the distant Portuguese colony of Mozambique, in Africa.

The entire de Voogd family survived the war and we met them in Nederland in 1946. Our uncle served as ambassador of the Netherlands in the Far East after the war, including Nanking, China, Canberra, Bangkok, Manila and finally Tokyo. Many years later, I stayed with the de Voogds at the Dutch embassy in Tokyo. I was on my way to Java to find my mother's grave and to visit our former nanny and her family.

Figure 9 Our home in Batavia just before the war, October, 1941. Our aunt Rins de Voogd and her boys have been evacuated from Japan by the Dutch Foreign Service. From left to right: Bert and Jan de Vries, 11 and 13 years old, Jan and Bert de Voogd, 9 and 7, Rins de Voogd-de Vries 38, Joan de Vries 9, Dr. Bert de Vries 40, Tine de Vries-Berg 43, and Jack de Vries 7.

Japan Attacks America

After the Japanese sneak attack on the US Navy fleet at Pearl Harbor on December 7th of 1941, the Netherlands joined America and Britain in declaring war on Japan. Our government believed that Java, Sumatra and Borneo would be safe because the mighty American armed forces in the Philippines and the British in Malaya and Singapore would form an impregnable "Malay Barrier." After all, our allies were the superpowers of the day, and we would be safe.

I had finished first grade before the war started. Second grade was cut short when the Japanese bombing began. During the air raids, the awful moan of the siren would send us all to the air raid shelter in the backyard. It was a slit-trench with rough wooden benches under a giant mango tree. The black-out was taken very seriously and we learned to find our way to the backyard shelter at night in the dark. It could have been more of an adventure if we weren't all so nervous about it. Nobody had any experience with war, bombing and rushing to air raid shelters in the dark with small home-made backpacks.

The Fall of Singapore

As outlined in the extensive literature about the war in the Pacific, the Western Allies were tragically ill-prepared for modern combat. Three days after the Japanese attack on Pearl Harbor, the Japanese Air Force sank the two mighty

British Navy battleships *Prince of Wales* and *Repulse* off Singapore, opening the way for the Japanese invasion fleets. The complacent British Army was decisively defeated on the Malay Peninsula and Singapore was taken from its largely undefended land side. The "Gibraltar of the East" fell into Japanese hands on February 15, 1942, stunning the Western Allies. With the fall of Singapore, the Japanese invasion fleets could now approach the Dutch East Indies at leisure. At the disastrous Battle of the Java Sea, the Japanese overwhelmed the 5 aging battleships and cruisers of the ABDA (American, British, Dutch, Australian) fleet with their superior long-range torpedoes. The Allies, bravely led by our own Admiral Karel Doorman, had no air cover and were fighting blind. They faced an overwhelming force of 6 modern aircraft carriers, 4 battleships, 8 heavy cruisers and a swarm of light cruisers and destroyers, who were escorting 97 Japanese troop transport ships, in two fleets. In the ensuing battle more than half of the Allied crews were killed. Only three Allied ships escaped this shocking disaster. The Japanese landed in several places along the northern coast of Java, as well as near Java Head, the northeastern cape of the island, facing Sumatra across the Sunda Strait. At the beaches north of Bandoeng there was some fighting, but the poorly trained and equipped Dutch Army soon collapsed. The Japanese had air supremacy, and we were totally and tragically unprepared for modern war.

Most of the European nations, as well as America, had become strongly pacifist after the horror and carnage of

World War I, and had cut military budgets to absurdly low levels. That understandable but naive idealism would lead to the death of millions of men, women and children worldwide. The massive military build-up in Germany and Japan had been ignored, only to be paid for in 'blood, sweat and tears.' No one had been willing to listen to Churchill's warnings.

Evacuation to the Countryside: Pandeglang

Our parents had heard the radio reports about the war in Europe and the bombing of Rotterdam, the fall of Paris and the bombing of London, so they expected that our capital city of Batavia, with its major harbor, would be heavily bombed by the Japanese. My parents decided to evacuate my older brother Bert, older sister Joan and me to the countryside where we would be safe. They sent us, accompanied by our wonderful nanny, Juffie, to live with Mr. and Mrs. Wijngaarden, who were friends of theirs living in the small crossroads town of Pandeglang, in the countryside west of Batavia. We addressed our hosts as "Oom Kees and Tante Jane" even though they were not actually uncle and aunt. Oom Kees (ohm case) was the Dutch Assistant Resident, the head of the Dutch civil government in Bantam province. They lived in a very large colonial house with many servants and stately grounds— the symbol of colonial power.

I remember the Pandeglang experiences very vividly, probably because I was such a scared little boy of 7. I remember the air raid sirens, the dark air raid shelter and the Japanese planes going overhead in the weeks before the invasion in early March of 1942. There was no Dutch Army presence to speak of. Then one afternoon, all of sudden, Japanese trucks with soldiers standing fully armed and with camouflage twigs on their helmets came roaring through town on their way to the provincial capital of Serang, further inland. There were groups of Javanese natives standing alongside the road cheering them on, and we were of course very scared and did not know what to expect. I remember saying: "Why are they waving to the Japanese? The Japs are our enemy." There was no battle and no Dutch armed resistance.

I learned only later that the educated elite among the natives on Java had long pressed for more independence from Dutch colonial rule. They got very few concessions from the rigid conservatives in Holland. In other parts of our enormous archipelago, the population was still loyal to Queen Wilhelmina. In fact, a sizable number of Christian natives from Menado and Ambon joined the Dutch Army and many insisted on being jailed as POW's along with their white fellow-soldiers. Even before the war, Japanese propaganda had promised independence from Dutch rule, with the slogan of "Asia for the Asians." But I didn't understand any of that at the time.

That afternoon, Oom Kees put on his full uniform, a white suit with gold braid, and sat on the front lawn of this imposing official residence. And while the Japanese trucks were rumbling by on the way to the provincial capital of Serang, there was an old Javanese man in a Dutch Army uniform who came up to Mr. Wijngaarden to ask for instruction on how to fight the enemy. He was an old soldier with medals on his shirt. Oom Kees apparently said "Thank you, but never mind, it is over." I remember being very upset that there was the dreaded enemy just roaring right by. There was no fighting, and there was apparently nothing to be done.

The next day, we were all told to stay indoors because there was going to be trouble. There were a lot of natives running all over the grounds stealing things, and we were kept in our bedroom with the wooden shutters closed. Then the Japanese walked in and immediately arrested Oom Kees. We were afraid and did not know how to behave, and neither did Tante Jane. We stayed in the house for a while and then were told the Japanese would use it as their headquarters. We were ordered to move across the central grassy common into the little Dutch hospital, where there was a Dutch nurse. Tante Jane, Juffie, Bert, Joan and I all moved into the little house with the nurse.

The Battle of the Sunda Strait

As it turned out, when we moved to Pandeglang, we had moved close to the Japanese invasion beaches on the Sunda Strait separating Java from Sumatra, about a half hour's drive over narrow, rough roads. The invading Japanese reached us before they reached Batavia. (There are a number of books about the Battles of the Java Sea and Sunda Strait and the unnecessary cruelty of the Japs toward the shipwrecked survivors. See the Bibliography.)

Out of the 5 Allied cruisers that began the Battle of the Java Sea, only 2 survived. After refueling in Batavia, they made a run for Australia, first westward to the Sunda Strait and then south. These were the heavy cruiser USS *Houston* and the light cruiser HMAS *Perth* and a Dutch destroyer named *Evertsen*. Without air reconnaissance to warn them, they ran right into one of the major Japanese invasion fleets. They fought desperately and did sink 4 Japanese troop ships out of 56, but they themselves were repeatedly torpedoed by the Japs and sank near midnight, with the loss of half their men. Some of the Australian and American seamen who survived the battle were brought to our little inland town of Pandeglang. Some were operated on in the small Dutch hospital, but most of them were put in the old Dutch jail. To make room for these POW's the Japs simply released all the native convicts.

We played inside the fenced hospital grounds and peeked out to see the Japanese doing military drills on the common—charging forward with their rifles and bayonets, yelling and then falling down, then charging again. When we saw them doing bayonet practice on dummies tied to posts, their yelling and violence scared us. We also saw the tired American and Australian Navy survivors walking under guard to and from the nearby jail in small groups.

39

Tante Jane asked my sister to take a pack of cigarettes to two of the Navy survivors who were sitting outside their rooms in the hospital compound. Bert and I went with her for support. We were told that these Navy men did not speak Dutch, so we were quite shy about approaching them, but they thanked us, and lit up right away.

Digging Graves in the Lawn

One of my most frightening memories is of these white prisoners in their tattered clothes being made to dig their own graves in the large front lawn of the Wijngaarden Resident's house we had just evacuated. When we saw the open graves, Bert, Joan and I ran back across the large grass park and covered our ears. But we still heard the rifle shots and cried in panic, not willing to believe that they had actually killed these Navy survivors.

(Neither the American nor the Australian books in the bibliography about the Battle of the Sunda Strait mention summary executions in Pandeglang.)

Perhaps these were mock executions, which the Japs also favored as a way of instilling fear in everyone. After a month or so, our nanny Juffie, Bert, Joan and I were released by the Japs and allowed to return to Batavia because all of the nearby jails were full of POW's. It was strange to find our mother and Jan living as before—as if nothing had happened. They had so far only glimpsed the Japanese soldiers marching around the city.

Dad had been called to the mountain city of Bandoeng by his superiors in the Ministry of Economic Affairs to join the nucleus of the retreating Netherlands East Indies government. Bandoeng had been proclaimed the "Mountain Fortress" that would be defended at all costs.

Dad told us later that our small Navy and Air Force did actually fight to the death, but their distant heroism was not seen by the native population. Unfortunately, our small Army's quick defeat was witnessed all too clearly by the native population, in the countryside and in the cities, on all the islands. Our defeat was used by the Japanese to discredit the Dutch as unworthy colonial rulers. The Japanese boasted they were liberating the rest of Asia and replacing the Europeans once and for all. "Asia for Asians!" was one of their propaganda slogans.

During the occupation, the Japanese government courted the nationalist Indonesian leaders. Sukarno was invited to Tokyo and promised autonomy for Indonesia within the "Greater East Asia Co-Prosperity Sphere." His collaboration with the Japanese enemy was to become one of the stumbling blocks after the war during peace negotiations between Indonesia and Holland.

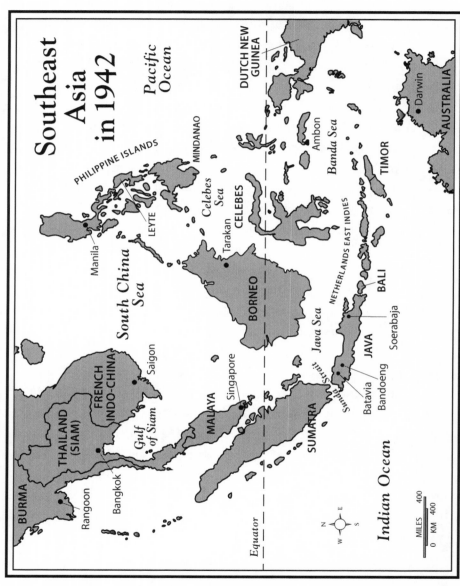

Map: Sharen Faye Design

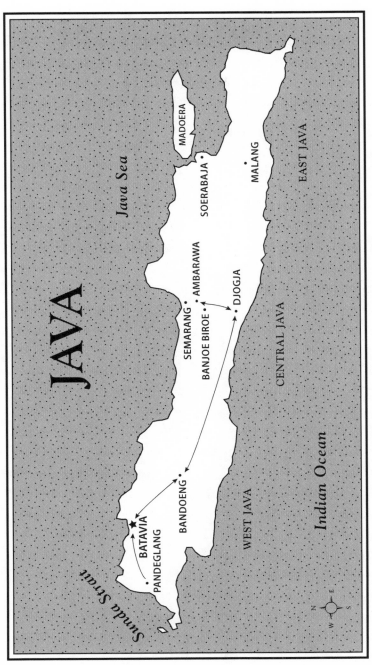

The island of Java is approximately 700 miles long and 75 miles wide.
Tropical and densely populated, it has 17 volcanoes and rich soil.

Map: Sharen Faye Design

Chapter Four

FORTRESS BANDOENG

After the three youngest kids and our nanny returned from the countryside, our family was reunited with Dad in Bandoeng. At the start of the Japanese occupation in early 1942, my father Bert de Vries was 41 years old and my mother Tine de Vries-Berg was 44. My brothers Jan and Bert were 13 and 11, while Joan and I were 9 and 7 years old.

As the Japanese invasion threatened, Queen Wilhelmina and her Dutch Government-in-Exile in London, had broadcast instructions to us: "No scorched earth defense. Safeguard essential equipment and services for the good of the population. Remain at your posts as long as the enemy will allow, and keep the wheels of society in motion."

As a result, Dad continued his work at the Ministry of Economic Affairs for the first year of Japanese occupation. In due time, even these senior Dutch civil servants (often called "Nippon workers") and their families were interned in Bandoeng. Because Juffie was Eurasian, she was not interned with us, and remained free throughout the war years. We were housed in a residential section of the city that had been fenced off and made into a camp. It was called the Flower Camp because before the war the streets had the names of various flowers. Our house was on the

Seringen Laan (Lilac Lane). We shared the house with
another Dutch family.

One of my memories about my Mom at this time was
that she developed an open wound on her leg that would
not heal. At that point no one was dying of starvation yet,
but seeing that her wound wouldn't heal left me a bit
worried—something was not quite right with my mother,
and she was the center of our world.

What Makes People Admirable?

One day, we were helping my mother to the house of
someone who dressed her wound. On the way home, Mom
had a brief conversation with a man I did not know. Ours
was a small camp of "Nippon-workers" where men were
allowed to remain with their families. Once we returned
from the clinic, Mom told me that the man she had spoken
with had been a famous and powerful figure on Java before
the war. But of course to me he looked just as ordinary as
all the other men in the camp.

We talked about the fact that a lot of these once rich
and powerful men were now no different from anyone else.
They had been stripped of everything they had come to
depend on and now they were just as helpless and as
anxious as everyone else.

Later on, in Kamp 10 and Kamp 7, I noticed that the
leaders in the camps were often not the older, once famous
leaders from before the war. Instead, the natural leaders

who emerged were younger people who voluntarily took on extra work and extra risk. They were chosen by their fellow prisoners because they were seen as totally honest and trustworthy. So those were the really admirable people— not the rich and famous "leaders" from before the war.

Empty Ghost Houses

In this family camp, it was eerie to explore the houses inside the barbed wire fence which we were not allowed to live in but which just stood there—still fully furnished, but empty. My brothers found out that a dog had been left behind in one of these empty houses and was barking frantically. I was scared to see this poor dog jumping and barking at us, while still tied to the leg of a heavy dining room table. We felt awful because we were afraid it would bite if we tried to free it. We did push a dish of water to the dog with a long stick. I believe my brothers reported this frantic dog to the guards who we thought would somehow take care of it. I don't know what happened to the dog. It has remained an awful memory.

At other times my sister and I would dare to explore these ghost houses ourselves. In one of them, we found everything intact—the table set and scraps of food still left on the plates. It was spooky. The family had apparently been arrested and rushed out of their house. They left everything behind except what they themselves could carry. One day, my sister and I found a beautiful oriental carpet in one of these ghost houses. We rolled it up and triumphantly carried it to "our house" in the Seringen Laan. Mom was upset that we had taken it. She said it did not belong to us, and made us take it back to the empty house.

Victorian Ethics

Because my mother was born in 1898 and my father in 1901, the religious and ethical values they grew up with were still quite Victorian. As best I can reconstruct the family values my parents grew up with (and of course passed on to us) they can be summarized as follows: *Try to be compassionate and tolerant; don't be judgmental. God is stern but also loving. Avoid blowing your own horn. Be modest and moderate in all you do and be thrifty.*

In the de Vries family education and intellect were highly prized. In fact, my grandfather de Vries had hoped to be a medical doctor, but his parents were not able to afford to send him to medical school. My father grew up within a rather strict and sober religious and ethical framework, quite in line with the prevailing Victorian ethics of the times.

In the literature on this topic it is clear that in Britain, as well as Holland, this set of social values often meant that the oldest sons would go into the Army, the Navy, Merchant Marine or the Church. This set of social values also included a decidedly anti-business bias. Businessmen were typically regarded as self-promoting people who took advantage of others—and of course there had been gross abuses during the late 1800's in all industrializing Western European nations as well as in America.

Among the de Vries and Berg families, there were a number of uncles who made their careers in the law, the military, the foreign service, clergy, merchant marine, and banking. Our maternal grandfather Roelof Harm Berg was a captain in the Royal Netherlands East Indies Army in the late 1800's. His entire family, including my mother Tine Berg, had lived on Java for decades. When he died of malaria in 1910, the family moved back to Holland. As mentioned earlier, our uncle Nico de Voogd was in the Dutch Foreign Service and stationed in Japan.

Given this inheritance, my siblings and I grew up in a climate that valued honesty, hard work and intellectual pursuits. We also grew up without any encouragement about going into business. By osmosis, we picked up the notion that the life of businessmen was not for us—those were the slick, unprincipled people who only cared about making money.

Money was almost more taboo as a topic of conversation than sex. We were Victorian in our mores. And what we today would label as social/political skills were seen as quite unimportant, if not downright suspect. My father never learned to drive, dance or swim. He found social recreation in bridge, tennis, and various church activities. The denomination most closely resembling our church is probably the Presbyterian Church.

For me, a strong faith in God was very important in my early years. This faith was especially crucial when I was on my own in Ambarawa Kamp 7, when I was most anxious and alone and when I prayed often and desperately. Looking back on it now, I realize how invaluable it was for all of us to believe so strongly that there was a God who would set things right again.

At Easter in Kamp 7, I was part of a large group of kids and men that came together outdoors. One of the men spoke to us and led us in prayer as if we were in a real church.

Dad Arrested by the Kempeitai

Without any warning, one day a car pulled up to our house in the Lilac Lane and Dad was arrested by the *kempeitai,* the infamous Japanese secret police. That made us all apprehensive but weighed especially heavily on Mom. She pretended that he might well come back, because he had never said anything to her about joining the resistance against the Japanese. The frightening rumors were that the secret police tortured its prisoners to make them talk and that they never came back.

During the first years of the occupation, there had been no space to jail all of the hundreds of thousands of Dutch civilians who the Japs felt had to be controlled and separated from the native population. They had quickly fenced off various residential neighborhoods in each of the major cities and moved two or three groups of women and their children into each house. So in this early period, we lived in houses with the furniture that had been left there by the original inhabitants, but without any native servants. The quality and quantity of our food was diminishing, but no one was starving to death yet. Proteins and sugars were the first to become scarce. It became clear that the pre-war supply of meat, eggs, butter, milk and sugar were being used to feed the Japanese occupation Army. This lack of protein would lead to the deaths of a great many military and civilian prisoners as the months stretched into years. Our stock-piled medical supplies were similarly diverted and denied to the Allied prisoners.

I remember our time in the Lilac Lane very clearly. Schooling of the children was forbidden. The Japs forbade us from meeting in any small groups, even for teaching. Meetings could be used for subversive plotting, they said.

So we had a lot of free time. The four de Vries kids all worked to dig up the lawns around the house in order to grow tomatoes, carrots and spinach. Although our older brothers bossed us around about the garden chores, my sister and I were praised by Mom for helping out.

One day we were warned that Japanese front-line troops headed for combat would be allowed into every house in the camp and would be free to take anything they wanted. So we set about trying to find hiding places for Mom's jewelry. This house had belonged to a family that was taken elsewhere and so was fully furnished when it was assigned to us and another family. It even had an aquarium which my brothers kept working. We kids thought that perhaps the Japs wouldn't think to look for jewelry in the sand of the aquarium bottom. We were right, Mom's jewelry was not taken. As kids we felt proud to have outwitted these rough soldiers.

We giggled secretly when one of them took a tennis racquet that was still in its wooden frame. What was he going to do with that?

Chapter Five

INTO THE PRISON CAMPS

As the months stretched into years, we no longer had information from the outside world and could not find out if the Allies were coming closer to free us. Hiding a radio was as dangerous as hiding a firearm—both were punished by beheading—so for us there was no news at all. After all the empty rumors of approaching liberation, we just lived from day to day, unable to make any plans.

We were completely unaware that the Americans had landed nearby in New Guinea and the Philippines in October of 1944. The Japanese Army in the East Indies now became alarmed and prepared for an American invasion. They responded by drastically concentrating all the civilians they had interned in the early years and placing them under military command, now officially as prisoners. We were all issued serial numbers which we had to wear on our shirts. Mine was "26320." This was a major turning point for all of us because our food and living conditions became much, much worse.

Take Only What You Can Carry

As a result of this increased alarm among the Japanese, in November of 1944, the women and children in our camp in

Bandoeng were told to come to the camp gate with only what they could carry. We didn't know why. We didn't know that the Americans had landed in the Philippines— that the Japs and Americans were locked in terrible battles just north of us.

My two older brothers were ordered to stay behind in the almost empty camp in Bandoeng, in Western Java. By now Jan was 16 and Bert was 14. Would they be moved later to another camp? Would it be worse? No one knew. We were living with a lot of anxiety. All the details of daily life were unpredictable, with no end in sight.

Carrying suitcases, backpacks and rolled mattresses, Mom, Joan and I were trucked to a rail siding and loaded onto a train with all the other women and children. From now on, we would learn to live without tables and chairs, normal beds, glasses, china or any other furniture. Mom carried her suitcase and a thin mattress she had reduced in size, for herself and Joan. She tied the mattress with some string to keep it rolled up. I carried a Boy Scout bed-roll, my father's old leather briefcase and a home-made backpack.

Once on the train, we were allowed to sit on the wooden benches and look out. The train wound through the mountains for many hours, then over broad plains and into more mountains. Because it was hot during the day, we opened the window and stuck our faces into the wind until the cinders stung our eyes. When the steam train stopped to get fuel and water, some of the mothers pointed to the bundles of sticks that were loaded as fuel instead of anthracite coal.

"Look, they are cutting down the tea plantations and using those bundles of sticks instead of coal. That means the war is going badly for them." For my sister and me it was an adventure to be in the outside world again and to see the open countryside we were passing through.

Overcrowded Jails

After a day and a night on the train, we arrived in the old garrison town of Ambarawa, in central Java. A scary half hour truck ride at night, standing tightly crowded against each other, had brought us all to Banjoe Biroe (bahn you beeru) Kamp 10, far out in the countryside. It had been designed long ago as a jail compound for native prisoners, surrounded by a tall white-washed brick wall with watch towers, and ringed with a watery moat.

This was the beginning of real imprisonment for us. We were allowed just enough space on wooden platforms and our own mattresses to lie on our backs—shoulder to shoulder. We all slept in our clothes. I don't recall seeing anyone in pajamas and there was no privacy. Some women tied strings to nails in the walls and hung shirts or towels to mark their family territory. This was a concentration camp in the literal sense of the word.

As an aside, I learned some years ago that concentration camps were first used by the British during the Boer War in the early 1900's. When the Boer women continued to shelter and supply their men in prolonged guerilla campaigns, Lord Kitchener herded them together in "concentration camps." His neglect of elementary sanitation led to epidemics of typhoid and dysentery. At least 20,000 died in history's first civilian concentration camps, mostly women and children. (See Pakenham, *The Boer War* in the bibliography.)

According to the literature on this subject, almost all of the civilian men, women and children who died in the Japanese camps like the ones I was in, died from hunger and disease in the final twelve months of their imprisonment. This is the time that most of us were so tightly concentrated in our camps. This is the time that our food got so much worse. The death rate rose exponentially from the time of the American landings in the Philippines in October 1944 to the first arrival of food and medicines in September/October of 1945. During this final year, my mother and my uncle both died from hunger, while my father nearly died.

In every prison camp, early every morning, all the women and children had to be counted by the Jap commander and his guards. This meant we had to line up outside each barracks or stable in rows of five, facing forward. Then came the command to bow: "Keirei"! So we all bowed to the Jap—there was no choice. The first person in each line then had to sound off military-style with the

THEY'RE COMING.....BUT WHO FIRST?

Figure 10 "They're coming, they must be close by now." M. G. Hartley.

Yes, indeed they're coming - both Death and the Allies! It is a life and death race, in which Death all too frequently beat even the B 29 bombers. On many a wooden cross in our cemetery, the inscription might well have been: "Too late!"

number of that little row in Japanese. This was called "Tenko" by the Japs but we called it "Appèl" after the French word for counting. So we learned to call out the number of each row in Japanese: "Ichi, Ni, San, Shi, Go".... and so on. Sometimes I stood at the head of the column and nervously yelled the number.

In addition to weeding the camp grounds, one of my jobs was to get wet garbage from a nearby guard house and feed it to the pigs in Kamp 10. These pigs belonged to the Jap commandant. For this special job, we needed to go back and forth to the guard house. We thought it was exciting to be allowed outside the walls, accompanied by an armed sentry.

In January 1945, the camp commander announced that all boys ten years old and older had to leave. So after only a few months, I was separated from my mother and sister and found myself on a truck with other boys, headed for Ambarawa and Kamp 7, where we found thousands of older, sickly civilian men.

When we heard that I had to leave, a friend of my mother's gave me a pencil drawing. Pictured opposite, it draws a parallel between the capable, can-do spirit of the Boy Scout song from before the war with the work we did with the cart and the heavy barrels, feeding the pigs. The message to me and to my mother was that I would be capable of handling what might lie ahead. I treasured this drawing and kept it safe in my children's bible through all the following turmoil.

Figure 11 Drawing given to me as I was leaving Banjoe Biroe.

Saved by the Atom Bombs

After the atom bombs had been dropped on Hiroshima and Nagasaki, on August 6 and 9, 1945, the Emperor of Japan gave his unprecedented radio address to all of his subjects on August 15, announcing the end of the war. Without admitting that Japan had been defeated, the Emperor told the Japanese nation that "We must bear the unbearable." The official Japanese surrender ceremony did not take place until September 2, on board the USS *Missouri* in Tokyo Bay. It was not until that date that the various Japanese generals were given orders by the Allies to safeguard the prisoners in all of the conquered territories, until they could be disarmed by the American, British and Australian troops.

In that six day interim, Emperor Hirohito narrowly escaped a military coup by fanatic militarists who wanted to continue the war to its suicidal end.

As mentioned earlier, the American Navy, Marines, Army and Air Force had by-passed the Dutch East Indies in their drive towards Tokyo. At terrible cost, they had driven the Japanese out of the Pacific Islands: Guadalcanal, New Guinea, the Philippines, Saipan, Okinawa and Iwo Jima. Once the Philippines were in American hands again, the US Navy had begun to starve Japan for the oil from Sumatra, Java and Borneo by torpedoing the tankers as they steamed north to Japan, in the straits between the Philippines and the Chinese coast. But we were not allowed any news in the camps and didn't know any of this.

Liberation and Chaos

For us in the East Indies, there were no signs of approaching liberation. Except for the lone plane dropping leaflets in January, there had been no Allied planes overhead, no sounds of artillery, and no hint of the approaching Japanese surrender. But worst of all, it also meant that there were no Allied soldiers to re-establish a semblance of law and order. So when the Japanese announced the end of the war to us on Java, what we experienced was chaos. We didn't know where our family members were and had no money to go anywhere. The first thing we wanted was more food.

Soon after my reunion with Joan, there was excited commotion in Kamp 10 because there was an advance party of British photographers taking pictures of us. One of these men was standing on the roof of a small truck with a movie camera. My sister and I were standing in line for the latrine, and we said to each other: "Oh look, they are taking pictures of us. Maybe someday we'll see those."

Many years later, indeed we saw the picture of us standing in line in a Dutch book about the civilian camps, and I have included it here (Fig. 12). We are among the kids at the far right in the photo.

We found out later that this reconnaissance party visited many Dutch civilian camps in central Java, and was led by Lady Mountbatten, the wife of the British supreme commander in the Far East.

61

Figure 12 This is the picture of the latrine line in Kamp 10, taken by Lady Mountbatten's camera crew right after we were freed in September 1945. Everyone is holding a small container of water. Joan and I are on the right in the shade.

As a political prisoner, Dad was not set free until September 17, more than a month after the Emperor's surrender speech. As one of the most senior civilian Government officials remaining alive in the Netherlands East Indies, my modest, unassuming father had been tortured and accused of leading a network of spies. By some miracle he had survived, and he began to search for his family.

A few days after his release, he appeared in Banjoe Biroe Kamp 10. He had a shaved head, a worn-out shirt several sizes too large and old khaki shorts. He was pale, emaciated and looked so strange—hardly recognizable, especially without any hair.

"Daddy, Daddy! Oh, oh.......you are here! Oh......" I flew into his arms and the tears came flooding out again, in grateful relief. "Are the boys all right? Where are they? Are they coming here too?"

All of a sudden, my distant and aloof, dimly-remembered father was now the new center of my world. I didn't really know him well, but now I clung to every word he said and followed him around the camp like a shadow. "I found the boys in Bandoeng and told them to wait for us there. We will soon be together again," he said.

But She Had Disappeared

Now one of the first things we did was to visit my mother's grave. Some of the women had been allowed to accompany coffins to the cemetery in town. They told Dad where the cemetery could be found. With an anxious pit in my stomach, Dad, Joan and I hitched a ride on a truck going to Ambarawa and walked to the old Dutch cemetery. Beyond the pre-war tombstones, we found a field with bare earth and many rows of wooden stakes. Each had a name and a date written on it in ink and we found hers. I cried and sobbed—bewildered—how could this be? Just a little piece of wood? She couldn't just disappear like this! But she had disappeared.

Now it was up to Dad to make sense of things again. I didn't know him nearly as well as I had known my mother.

63

Sunset Over Java

He was a Victorian professor who wasn't expected to do things with his children, or even to talk with them that much. Even my older brothers never learned any sports from him, and he was uninterested in fixing mechanical problems. Now I needed him to be my friend and coach and craved his attention.

Chapter Six

FIGHTING FOR TIME

Dad began to tell us about his 15 months in the hands of the secret police. They had interrogated him day after day, pressing him to name other men who might have done subversive things against the Jap regime. They had beaten him, often several times a day, and given him the "water treatment"—bringing him close to drowning and letting him revive. Then the questions, the beatings on his head and knees, and the drowning again. In order to stall for time, he had begun to make up stories about sabotage and espionage, but naming only those men who had already been caught early in the occupation and beheaded.

The Japanese had eliminated each small group of civilians who had worked together. In the Japanese way of thinking, any organized resistance had to have had an overall leader. No group of Japanese individuals would act on their own initiative like that, so there had to be a leader. They continued to torture my father to reveal the name of that leader.

"But You Want to Die"

When a former colleague yelled out in agony that my father had indeed plotted against the Japs in order to save himself from further beatings and water boarding, Dad feared that he too might break under torture and implicate innocent men. One night, in desperation, he tried to commit suicide. He smashed his glasses and took a piece of a lens and cut his wrists. But the guards found him still alive and rushed him to a hospital. He was watched around the clock and in the middle of the night one of the Japanese officers said, "Well, you are a criminal. You know we are torturing people to extract facts from them, and we succeed because people want to live. But you want to die. Now if you have really written off your life, there is a chance you will keep it."

Then Dad realized that he might stop his own suffering and that of other suspects if he named himself as the resistance leader. He thought that as long as he told them about a lot of imagined spying, they would need him alive.

Leader of the Resistance

After some days had passed, Dad was brought in for interrogation again. They said "We know that before the war, you worked in the Ministry of Economic Affairs and that your boss was Dr. van Mook. We also know that he is now the head of the Dutch East Indies Government in Australia. Now admit it—you are the leader of the underground movement here on Java!" That close connection with van Mook was incriminating.

"Yes—you are right," he said. "I cannot resist you any longer." They were triumphant and said, "We knew all of this six months ago. Now give us your confession in detail."

That led to months of further questioning while he made up elaborate stories of espionage that involved sending coded messages to the Allies through Tokyo's own Foreign Service. Now that they had "discovered" the head of all resistance, they thought Dad would have a great deal of valuable information. The Japs were insatiable for information and wrote everything down in Malay, long-hand. That information was then translated into Japanese. That took still more time, which was what Dad was fighting for.

After some months of spinning elaborate espionage stories, Dad was brought in to face the head of the political department of the Kempeitai, named Iasaki. He said to my father, "We have checked all your stories and we now realize you have been playing a game with us. I am in Foreign Affairs and we are not as stupid as you think we are. We have gone through all the files in Tokyo and not one of your coded messages to the Allies is there. You have been lying to us all these months."

The next morning, he was brought before Iasaki again, and Dad told him that it was true that he had made up the stories about leaks from Japanese officers secretly relayed to the Allies, and about his being the head of all resistance. Iasaki was incredulous and asked why Dad had confessed to things he had not done. Dad explained that he was tortured and beaten for so many months that he had to confess to espionage stories, even if the stories were not true. Iasaki said, "But you could have been beheaded after your confession." Dad had replied, "Yes, but I might have been killed anyway. You have killed many people who have done nothing against you, so what difference does it make?"

Then Iasaki said, "Why do you recant now?" "But Sir, you are the first superior intellect in the Japanese secret service that I have met." "Ah," he said, "Your life will be safe if you stick with me. If you persistently deny your guilt, I will save your life."

While working in the government office in Bandoeng that first year of the occupation, my father's crime had been to divert some funds from the Japanese Army. He had secretly distributed these monies to the widows of Dutch soldiers who had been left with no income. That was a crime against the Japanese Government, and in their eyes had to be part of a wider network of sabotage and resistance. But he had not been the head of any resistance network and had never been involved in espionage for the Allies.

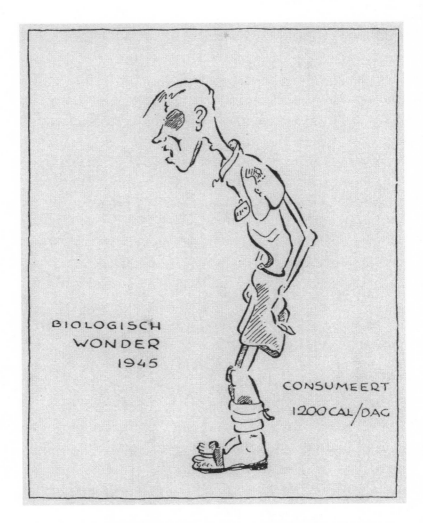

Figure 13 **"Biological Miracle 1945. Consumes 1200 calories per day."**

Note: This and a number of similar line drawings were made by Mr. M. G. Hartley in Bob Zweede's camp in Tjimahi. I have translated his sardonic notes. Note the legs swollen by scurvy.

Fifteen Years in Prison

Eventually, when Dad was sentenced he found that Iasaki had kept his word. He was not sentenced to death—but to a further fifteen years in prison. Under the circumstances, with disease and starvation rampant, all such sentences were equivalent to the death sentence anyway. In the next jail, he did almost die and was brought to the Death Ward from which only he and a small Chinese prisoner emerged alive. The others all died from hunger, disease and neglect. A lot of them had dysentery and scurvy. The tops of their bodies were emaciated while their legs were swollen.

To get relief from his scurvy, Dad had asked one of the orderlies to bring him the weeds growing between the cobblestones in the prison yard. He ate them raw for their vitamins and gradually began to revive.

In time he learned that the prison had a store room full of tapioca flour from the nearby plantations for which there probably wasn't enough transport. He also found out that the infirmary had a supply of sulfuric acid. From his school days in Holland he remembered that a combination of flour and sulfuric acid could produce glucose. When he was allowed to produce this sugary glucose for those most in need, he was promoted to head of the central kitchen. In that position, he was able to surreptitiously divert various foods to the most seriously ill inmates. To hide this from the Jap commander, he made up elaborate fictitious reasons for the spoilage of the stored materials.

During these first days and weeks that Dad was with us in Kamp 10, he told us a number of stories about his interrogations and torture, and they made a strong impression on us. My sister and I hung on Dad's every word and were left in awe of his tenacity, cunning and brainpower. Many years later, I asked him to let me record his memories of this critical time in his life.

Figure 14 For our family memoir, I recorded extensive oral histories with Mother and Dad, 1977.

Oral Histories

In 1977 I interviewed my father and step-mother about their early lives in the East Indies and their experiences in the camps on Java. I did this so that my daughter Margot

71

and all of my nieces, nephews and cousins growing up in peacetime USA would have a chance to understand how the de Vries and Zweede families came together in Indonesia and in the Netherlands.

The 20 hours of taped interviews were eventually transcribed for the book *War Came to Java*, a private printing which I put together in 1998 with the help of many family members. My father's interrogation and torture by the Japanese Secret Police is recounted there in detail in his own words.

Chapter Seven

WAR CAME TWICE

During the week that our father was making arrangements to travel back to West Java with us, he also made some visits to women whose husbands had died at times and places he could tell them about. I went with him on these visits. He told me there was a lady in Kamp 10 who had grown up in his home town in Holland and that he knew where her husband had died. He had not been beheaded. Her name was Lexie Zweede (Zwayduh) and she had been elected to be the head of her large barracks in Kamp 10, and eventually the entire camp. She had earned the love and respect of the other women and children for her integrity and leadership. Her husband, Jan Zweede, had been a coffee plantation manager before the war. They had lived on the slopes of a volcano in East Java and had three children, Bob, Annelies and Johan. These brief visits were of course very sad—everyone weeping and trying to comfort one another.

In the meantime, our food was beginning to improve. There were days when we would hear airplanes approaching, and we would rush outside to see the parachutes come down with all kinds of canned foods and medicines. That was still the only contact with the Allies. The big planes were marked with the Dutch colors and we

Figure 15 Who can describe the emotions and joy we experienced upon seeing our Red, White and Blue flag on the planes as they dropped medical supplies and food. For some these made the difference between life and death. M. G. Hartley.

waved and cheered wildly every time they flew low over the camp.

A Lawless Countryside

This was tangible help from the outside world, but there was still no sign of any British or American troops. There was no new Dutch government and no police to keep order. Our Dutch soldiers had all been imprisoned as POW's in 1942, and had been taken to Thailand and Burma or to the mines of Japan as expendable slave laborers. Meanwhile, all of the Japanese garrisons were waiting to be disarmed. But the British were still mostly in Burma.

After a few days, Dad told us we were taking the train back to Bandoeng where our brothers were waiting for us. We climbed aboard a truck leaving for the town of Ambarawa and found ourselves at the train station in the late afternoon. There was a Dutch man with a Red Cross armband keeping a record of the whites who were coming and going. He warned Dad that there were "disturbances in the interior" where the Indonesians were establishing a movement designed to prevent the return of the Dutch Government, by force if necessary. Sukarno had declared independence and created the Republic of Indonesia. The Japanese occupation had ended, but no effective government had taken its place as yet. There was no police or Army—it was a lawless countryside, holding its breath.

In the middle of the night, a west-bound train pulled in to the station, and in spite of the warning, we climbed aboard. The train was filled to overflowing with Indonesians, with only a few white faces. We sat in a small compartment, and as the sun came up we looked out over the countryside—how wonderful to see open landscapes again. Dad had apparently been able to buy some hard-boiled eggs and I got an entire half all for myself. In late afternoon we arrived in Djogjakarta, which would become the headquarters for Sukarno and his fanatic young men fighting the Dutch. The city was a sea of red and white republican flags. But we checked into the railroad hotel and Joan, Dad and I had an entire room, with a big bathroom, all to ourselves. My sister went around and marveled at the luxury of it all—an entire bathroom, just for us? We also found real beds, with real sheets and mosquito nets and we had dinner in the restaurant.

There was another Dutch couple from Ambarawa, the Reverend and Mrs. de Jong. She had tried to keep an eye on my sister in Kamp 10 after my mother died. They thought they could now go back to live in their home in a nearby town because the war was over. They lived to regret that assumption.

Murderous Slogans

Dad was in an optimistic mood concerning the Indonesian celebration all around us. He brought back some "satay" from a native street vendor who had told him that the Japs had taken away all of the water buffalo which they needed to plow the rice paddies. He was happy to see "these damn Japs" go. He said that the Indonesian people were happy to have us, the Dutch, back in charge. What about all those murderous slogans we saw painted on the sides of the railroad cars? What did they mean by "Merdeka" and "Asia Raya?" ("Independence" and "Asians, wake up and rise")

And what about all these strange red and white flags? Why are they not the Dutch red, white and blue flags? Where had all of these large flags come from so quickly?

Before the war, Dad had been part of a group of so-called "Political Progressives" who favored an accelerated economic and political integration of natives and whites. Such a more liberal political transition had been put in place successfully by the Americans in the Philippines. Because of his political views, Dad had been denied a seat in the pre-war cabinet by the arch-conservative businessmen and plantation owners. They regarded him as too liberal and anti-business in his political views.

Being in sympathy with the Indonesians, Dad now assured us that the natives meant us no harm and were simply celebrating the end of the war. The next day, after an all-day train ride, we finally arrived in Bandoeng at dusk. There we were immediately met by a Dutch civilian armed with a rifle. This stranger was very concerned about us and asked if we were all right—had we had any trouble from the natives? He asked where we were going. Dad said that his two sons were waiting for us in the large Fifteenth

Battalion camp. We walked the dark streets of Bandoeng with this man and his rifle, and I very quickly picked up the feeling of real apprehension in the air. Wasn't it safe to walk without an armed guard now that the war was over?

All too soon we began to hear stories of white women and children being murdered as they left the camps to go home. It was later confirmed that we had indeed been the last white passengers allowed to remain alive on that train trip from Central to West Java. This was anarchy and it was frightening.

A New Nightmare

So we were "free"—but now we were huddled in the 15th Battalion camp, and all of a sudden the end of the war we had all dreamed about was turning into a new nightmare. Two days after the Japanese surrendered, Sukarno had declared Indonesia an independent republic. Now he had a golden opportunity because there were still no Allied troops to disarm the Japanese or to restore any law and order.

During the occupation, the Japanese Army had trained thousands of natives as para-military soldiers. They had indoctrinated them to despise the Dutch and held out the promise of self-government within the Japanese Empire once the Allies had sued for peace. Many of these so-called "Heihos" had served as our camp guards.

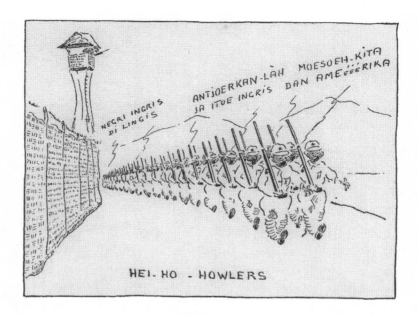

Figure 16 **The Indonesian soldiers whom the Japanese called "Heihos," depicted by Hartley as they march past his camp. They are singing songs that boast of the defeat of the English and Americans.**

When these native soldiers heard that the Japanese had surrendered and were waiting for the British troops to arrive from Burma, they saw their chance to seize power before the Dutch colonial government could return. They surrounded a Japanese garrison near Soerabaja (Surabaya) and demanded the Japanese weapons. Once they had armed themselves, they threatened other garrisons and soon were in control of East and Central Java. Within weeks they had some 20,000 Dutch civilian hostages there. In West Java, where we were, the young fanatics were still biding their time.

Here in Bandoeng, as I wandered around the 15th Battalion Camp, I found empty match boxes with colorful propaganda images aimed at the native population. Wooden matches and matchboxes are rarely seen nowadays, but that is all there was in those years.

These rare examples of war-time Japanese propaganda are part of this book's cover. They show Roosevelt and Churchill as defeated cowards, running away and holding their broken ships and planes. Roosevelt and Churchill are shown clinging to a raft, with the periscope of a Japanese submarine nearby. Others show Japanese tanks and planes dominating the world of the Allies, indicated by the British, American and Chinese flags. Japanese scissors are shown cutting the chains of oppression, freeing Asian peoples from Chinese, British and American rule. The slogans on these matchbox covers are in Malay. "Tentoe Dapat Kemanangan" means "Certain to Win Victory." Others say "Look How Strong We Are" and "Step on our Enemy."

A Dangerous Power Vacuum

Throughout the three and a half years of war, the British military had been fighting long and bloody battles in Asia. They had barely stopped the Japanese from invading India and were fighting over difficult jungle terrain to re-take Burma.

When the secretly-developed atom bombs brought the war to such an unexpectedly early end, neither the British nor the American armies were prepared to send troops to re-establish law and order in the distant Dutch East Indies. There had been no preparations to occupy such a large archipelago. Once the Japanese had surrendered, MacArthur and Mountbatten agreed that the Dutch East Indies should be liberated and stabilized by the British.

When the Japanese surrendered to the Allies in early September 1945, they were instructed to maintain law and order in all of the conquered territories under their control and to safeguard their prisoners until such time as the widely-scattered Japanese forces could be disarmed by Allied troops. Unfortunately for us, the former Netherlands East Indies had been by-passed by the Americans on their way to conquer Japan and had not yet been reached by the British, who were moving from their bases in India in their attempt to re-conquer Burma and Malaya. As a result, there were no Allied troops nearby to disarm the Nipponese troops on Java, Sumatra or Borneo. It took six weeks before the first British Army units reached us in Bandoeng. This power vacuum was an ideal opportunity for the Indonesian nationalists to seize control of the country and thereby prevent the return of the Dutch Government authorities.

The British military commanders charged with disarming the Japanese troops in the Dutch East Indies, therefore faced a number of nearly-impossible tasks: 1) locate and disarm the Japanese, 2) locate, feed and evacuate the civilian and military prisoners, and 3) maintain law and order without antagonizing the virulent Indonesian nationalists who soon saw the British as hand-maidens for the return of the Dutch Government's colonial rule.

In their attempt to sabotage the return of the Dutch government, Sukarno's young Indonesian fanatics began kidnapping and murdering the white civilians as they left the camps to return to their homes. This so-called *bersiap* revolution began with small groups of educated natives led by Sukarno and Hatta. As the months dragged on without any new government in place, the nationalistic fervor had time to grow, mainly on Java. In time, even the more mature nationalist leaders were unable to stop the kidnapping and killing carried out by their undisciplined young *pemuda* terrorists. We later heard that the Reverend and Mrs. de Jong were captured by the natives on the way to their pre-war home. Dad told us later that these friends of his were humiliated and brutally treated, but survived and eventually made it to Holland.

Back to the Camps

As a result of this Indonesian Revolution, we were all strongly urged to return to our camps. Was there supposed to be safety in numbers? Was the barbed wire fence going to keep us safe?

My father, my sister and I had moved in with my two older brothers, who had found bunks in one of the barracks in the 15th Battalion Camp in Bandoeng. There was a bulletin board near the camp gate where people had posted letters from family members elsewhere on Java, with warnings about the native fanatics who were now arming themselves and kidnapping some of the Dutch civilians who were leaving their camps to go home. There were frightening stories of white women and children being killed. Just as tragic was the fate of many Indonesians who were seen as being friendly to the Dutch, and who were also killed without mercy.

It was now October of 1945 and I was given a book for my eleventh birthday. It was an adventure story about a boy who finds a treasure, and I in turn treasured it as a new possession. The well-used book was a present from the Catholic Brother who had begun some very informal teaching for a small group of kids like me. We began with basic grammar and some very primitive arithmetic, but notepaper was scarce. All the other kids had also missed about three years of school. We would have a lot of catching up to do.

One of my vivid memories is of the four de Vries kids lying around on the stacked bunks in one of the half-empty barracks and passing around to one another an old tennis ball can, which we used to store the precious sugar we had somehow bought or bartered for. My brothers had also scrounged a large silver spoon which we used to scoop up a wonderful mouthful of sugar. We craved sugar and just couldn't get enough of it. Later on, a truck came into the camp with Australian mutton. These were large cans and we gorged on this incredible quantity of meat—real meat at last.

After a few weeks, we were warned that the Indonesian "extremists" were preparing to over-run the camp. Would they attack us with machetes or would they shoot us? I was really very frightened and tried to think of a place to hide. Perhaps I could hide inside one of those old, round galvanized garbage cans, and ask someone to put the lid on it. The natives did not attack our camp, and soon after that we heard that an advance guard of British troops was coming to protect us.

Rescued by the British Army

With great excitement we lined the avenue leading from the train station to our camp. We saw jeeps and trucks coming down the street that looked very different from the Japanese vehicles. The soldiers were brown-skinned Gurkhas, led by white British officers. Their uniforms and their equipment were all so different, and we were relieved when they established a defensive perimeter around our camp. We heard that these Gurkha troops had been stealthy fighters in the jungles of Burma and were feared by the Japanese. As part of their camouflage uniforms, they carried large curved daggers in their waistbands. We were wide-eyed and full of admiration. The stories went around about how these Gurkhas had climbed trees in Burma and silently killed Jap sentries by dropping their daggers from above.

The Gurkhas were from Nepal and did not understand my Dutch questions. I wanted to know where they had fought and how long it took them to reach us here in Bandoeng. They had set up guard posts outside the camp. Through the barbed wire fence, one of them gave me my first piece of chocolate. I thanked him with a big grin.

After some time, Dad felt it was safe enough to leave the camp, and so we moved into an empty house nearby. Soon my father was going off on various projects for the fledgling Dutch East Indies Government. In January of 1946, his former mentor, Dr. van Mook, persuaded him to return to Batavia to plan the distribution of essential food supplies. Because I was the youngest of the four kids, he decided to take me with him. The others were to continue some make-shift education.

When the time came, we couldn't go by train or by car because the Indonesian terrorists had blocked the roads and railroads and completely surrounded the city of Bandoeng. The Gurkha troops had fought a fierce battle to keep the airfield in Allied hands, and so Dad and I were airlifted out by the British.

Chapter Eight

AIRLIFT OUT OF BANDOENG

It was my first airplane ride, and it was on a DC-3 Dakota cargo plane, which sat on the field with its tail lower than its head. We scrambled up the sloping aluminum floor and sat on a bench, lengthwise to the plane. As we took off, the plane was shot at by rifles, and that produced some white-knuckle moments for me. But soon we were on the ground in Batavia, and I was told that it was indeed Dr. van Mook who was welcoming my father at the airport. Upon his return from exile in Australia, Dr. van Mook had been appointed acting Governor General of the Netherlands East Indies.

Things got even better when we moved into the house of the mayor of our capital city of Batavia. Mr. Boogaardt had also been jailed by the Japanese Secret Police, had been tortured in the same jails, and owed a debt of gratitude to my father. My father and I were warmly welcomed by Mr. and Mrs. Boogaardt, and I marveled at living in a normal house again with indoor plumbing, with real furniture, sleeping in my own bed and having plenty to eat.

Because Dad and I were still wearing our worn-out camp clothes, Mrs. Boogaardt arranged for new clothes for us. I was very proud of my new shirt and shorts, which I wore when an identity card photo was required. Dad also acquired some new clothes, including a coat and tie.

Figure 17 Identity card picture of my father and me in Batavia, early 1946. We are wearing our new clothes.

I was eleven years old now and had only a faint memory of first grade in school before the war. I struggled with basic spelling and grammar and had an especially difficult time remembering the multiplication tables, much as I tried. My anxiety was too high for school work—everything was so unsure without my Mom.

In the early months of 1946, I began to receive some lessons from a group of Dutch women who set up an improvised school in one of the private homes not too far away. This meant walking the streets of Batavia and being surrounded by brown skinned Indonesian natives. Before the war we had seen the natives as our friends. Certainly the servants in our house before the war were always very kind. Now all these native faces on the streets were faces I no longer dared to trust.

A Large City of Angry Natives

One of my blond classmates lived with his family in the street next to mine, and we often walked together to our classes. One day he was not there. Then I heard that he had been kidnapped and that his body had been found face down in the river. That was frightening to me—very frightening.

We began to hear that the majority of the troops guarding us here in Batavia were Sikhs from British India, while the Gurkha advance troops in Bandoeng had been Hindu. These Sikhs were Muslims and they began to sympathize with the Muslim natives seeking to prevent the return of the Dutch Government. They themselves were seeking independence from Britain. We heard that the English officers were now more and more reluctant to lead these Sikhs into any firefights with the natives and that some people had been kidnapped while the Sikh sentries looked the other way. In a way this became even more frightening than the camps had been because life in the camps had been structured with many rules. This revolution was unstructured and completely unpredictable. We were immersed in a large city of angry natives now. In a very real sense, war had come twice.

One evening our host, mayor Boogaardt, joined us at the dinner table and, patting his handgun, said how good it was to have seen fresh Dutch soldiers coming down the gangplank at the harbor. "This morning I saw those blond boys coming off their ships. Now we can finally trust our own sentries not to look the other way when one of us is being kidnapped." That was not lost on me, but I still didn't feel safe by myself on the streets. Those blond soldiers were still few and far between.

Free but also Penniless

After a while Dad and I began to wonder what had happened to the house we had lived in here in Batavia before the camps. When we found the house at New Tamarind Lane 20, it was completely empty. Every room was bare. There was not a stick of furniture left. The looters had all the time in the world once we were gone. A quick look in the garage confirmed what we suspected—the car was gone too. The front and back yards were deserted and the weeds were knee-high.

It became obvious that the Indonesians had helped themselves to all our belongings once we disappeared into the camps. Of course we had been forced to leave almost everything behind. For some of the Javanese natives this was no doubt a good motivation to support the new Republic of Indonesia—they didn't plan to give anything back to us if and when we returned from the camps. The Japs had quickly impounded all vehicles on every island in the archipelago for their own use, and now the natives took them anywhere they found them. We never saw our car again, nor any of our furniture. We were literally penniless.

What about savings? What happened to our family's bank account? Dad told me the Japs had simply taken over

Figure 18 Single guilder bills printed during the war. At first the Japanese printed them in Dutch, then in Malay, and finally the Dutch government printed its own with the Queen's portrait after we were freed from the camps.

all the banks when they began the occupation. And as I learned much later, all banks and insurance companies have a clause that holds them harmless in case of "war or insurrection." Well, we had all experienced the first and now we were in the middle of the second. Even the insurance on Mom's life was cancelled in Holland. The Japanese occupation Army had printed its own paper money and it remained in circulation for a while although now technically worthless.

Everyone's pre-war savings were simply gone. Our family was fortunate that our Dad was now beginning to earn newly-issued Dutch money as a valued senior economist in the fledgling Netherlands East Indies government.

Lexie Zweede

Soon after we moved in with the mayor and his wife, to my complete astonishment my father began to visit Mrs. Zweede, the woman he had met in Kamp 10 a few months ago. I had accompanied him then on the tearful visit when he told her how and where her husband had died. Mrs. Alexandrine (Lexie) Zweede was now recovering in a former prison camp in Batavia with her three children, waiting to be evacuated to the Netherlands. Their camp was on the other side of the city and was quite a long bicycle ride away.

Not only was I shocked that my father would have such an interest in this strange lady, but also I could tell that she really didn't want him around. She said later that she didn't want any man courting her. She was still mourning her late husband and trying to manage from day to day with her three children. Soon after she heard that the war was over, she received word that her husband had died of starvation in another camp. She was devastated......so devastated that she didn't want to live anymore and refused to eat when she was brought to a hospital complex in a nearby city. Only when her son Bob wrote her a letter begging her to choose life did she begin to eat again.

Her oral history of this episode is dramatic and compelling. It is included in our family book *War Came to Java* (see the Annotated Bibliography). When their hospital complex was surrounded by armed gangs of native fanatics threatening to kill them, Mrs. Zweede, Annelies and Johan were rescued in a daring and costly raid by the British Army. Five year old Johan Zweede had come very close to dying of hunger in Kamp 10, just before the Japanese surrender. He was dangerously emaciated.

Lexie's friends who had remained huddled in Kamp 10 told her later that they were attacked with mortars by the natives and defended by the Japanese garrison. So the hated Japanese helped save the lives of the Dutch women and children who had been their prisoners. The world turned upside down.

According to the official Dutch Army reports, at least 100 British soldiers gave their lives to rescue a total of 28,000 Dutch civilian hostages from numerous camps in Central Java. All had to be brought to the coast under military protection and evacuated to Batavia by ship, including Lexie, Annelies and Johan Zweede.

Lexie's oldest son Bob, who had come to find his mother and siblings, was ordered to return to his camp near Bandoeng. With help from my father, he traveled on the same "Last Safe Train" that we had been on.

It is estimated that approximately 2500 civilian ex-prisoners in central Java who went home early were kidnapped by the native extremists and were eventually declared missing and presumed dead. (See the various Dutch publications in the Appendix.)

Chapter Nine

SUNSET OF OUR LIVES

The infamous Japanese battle flag had featured the red rays of a rising sun and they had called their country "Dai Nippon," the Land of the Rising Sun. Because of the American atom bombs, their sun had now suddenly set in a dramatic way.

Figure 19 Japan's "Rising Sun" flag is red on white.

Coming out of the Japanese prison camps, we all thought we would return to re-start our previous lives. That was the happy life we remembered. After all, it was the only normal life we could imagine.

Instead, as some people dared to leave the Japanese camps, they found that some of the radical Indonesians now hated us. As a bewildered eleven year old, I found all of this turmoil more and more frightening. What was going to happen now? Why weren't we going home to begin a normal life again—with plenty of food, beds, and furniture?

Sunset of our Way of Life

The sunset of our way of life had begun in the Japanese prison camps. Now the native terrorists were making it final by killing innocent white survivors. This would be the end of my family's life on Java. Our interim government told us we could no longer be protected from the native terrorists. We had to flee. It was becoming too dangerous to stay.

As my brother Jan wrote in a brief memoir: "World War II was over, but the killing and fighting was not. British troops had taken command of the Japanese garrisons, but Dutch control was challenged by the Indonesian 'freedom fighters'—some well-organized, others no more than armed youngsters intent on loot and murder."

In April of 1946, my father, Bert, Joan and I were evacuated to Nederland by air. Our oldest brother Jan remained behind in order to complete his final exams. He was evacuated a few months later by ship, along with most of the other civilian survivors. Even though he had also lost three years of school, he managed to somehow pass the very demanding, all-important final exams. Upon his return to Nederland, Jan was admitted to the Medical School at the famous University of Leiden. It was an amazing feat.

Just before we left for the airport, we were invited to the downtown palace in Batavia by Dad's mentor, who was now the acting Governor General of the new Netherlands East Indies government. Dr. van Mook and his wife were very kind to us kids. I had only glimpsed this huge white-washed palace complex from a distance before the war. Now we were admitted by the guards and had tea on one of the enormous verandas with large potted palms. I was on my best behavior.

The flight from Batavia to Amsterdam remains a vivid memory for me because it was such a dramatic experience. We flew on a Skymaster. This four-engine propeller plane was flown by a Royal Dutch Air Force crew. The trip took five and a half days. For one thing, the crew had to sleep every night, and the plane had limited fuel capacity. After takeoff, our first stop was in Singapore where the airfield had been destroyed and re-built with steel matting for runways. You could see that the clay underneath the open metal grates was orange-brown—quite strange. Our first night was in Rangoon, Burma, where wrecked Japanese planes lined the runways – also quite strange. The second day we refueled in Calcutta and spent the night in Karachi. I remember seeing my first camel on the road from the airport. The next day we had lunch in steaming-hot Basra, Iraq, and arrived in Cairo for the night.

King Farouk's Palace

By now my anxiety about kidnapping and the Indonesian Revolution was probably beginning to diminish a bit, perhaps because we were lodged in one of King Farouk's former palaces. The Heliopolis palace had been taken over by the British during the war and was run as a very posh hotel, with red carpets, tall marble columns, and rose gardens. We were served quail by waiters in imposing uniforms. We giggled about the difficulty of finding any real meat on these little birds.

The next day, the four of us took the streetcar to see the Pyramids and Sphinx at Giza. Dad said he had pocket money of only a few piasters, so we just shook our heads to the Egyptian guides, but seeing the Sphinx and the Pyramids was an exciting treat.

We were also provided with our first warm clothing, courtesy of the Canadian Red Cross. I received woolen clothes I had never seen before. They felt scratchy. A woolen cap and woolen "plus-four" trousers, woolen socks and new shoes. Flannel underwear too. How strange. One surprise after another.

But before we got to the airport very early the next morning, I had a fright I still remember vividly. My father, brother and sister had gotten on a bus for the airport, but we got separated, and I found myself in the lobby of this grandiose palace by myself in the dark. At just 11 years old and speaking not one word of English, I was in a panic. I remember crying my eyes out, facing one of the monumental pillars in the lobby and getting more upset every time someone spoke to me in English trying to help me. After a while, my father must have noticed I wasn't on the bus and came back to get me. I was one upset and gun-shy little guy.

A New Life in Nederland in 1946

The next day we stopped for fuel in Naples and arrived at Amsterdam's airport in the afternoon. My paternal grandparents met us at Schiphol airport and brought us to their modest home in the town of Goes (approximately "hoose") in the southern province of Zeeland (zay lahnd). For the first few months, Bert, Joan and I made ourselves at home in the attic. On the floor below we found a bathroom without a bathtub. There was a toilet and a wash-stand with a pitcher of cold water, a large bowl and a washcloth.

All the strangers we met on the street in Goes were white. In contrast to the anxiety I had felt on the streets of Batavia, I slowly began to realize I didn't have to be afraid anymore. After we settled in a bit, I clearly remember walking the narrow brick streets of this ancient town with my grandfather de Vries, consciously relieved that everyone was European.

My grandfather ("Opa") de Vries was the retired preacher of the enormous "Great Church" that still dominates the town's skyline. It was completed in 1428 as a Catholic cathedral. After the Reformation it became the well-attended Protestant church of Goes. As we walked the streets, my grandfather was recognized and greeted by most everyone. That was a new experience for me. I had never lived in such a close-knit community, where people knew each other so well. Batavia had been far too large a city for that kind of personal recognition.

The important thing was that my family finally felt safe. It also meant that we were in a completely different world of cold weather, small houses with narrow staircases, tiny yards, brick pavements, different trees and different foods. Food was still rationed. Thank heavens at least we all spoke Dutch as we began to make the many adjustments that were needed in this new European world. After arriving in the spring of 1946 we all began to go to school.

Culture Shock

To make sure I would be warm enough my grandmother de Vries knitted white woolen underwear for me. It felt coarse and itched like crazy. I dutifully thanked her for it, but wore it as little as possible. The European winter of 1946/47 was the coldest in living memory. All the schools in Goes were closed for five weeks because there was not enough fuel to heat the buildings. We had time off, so the tropical de Vries kids all learned to skate. As a medieval town, Goes had been defended with walls, gates and a moat. The moat had been preserved and now made for a long ice skating park. The cold was miserable, especially for us coming from Indonesia.

After the first few months with our grandparents, Bert, Joan and I were generously invited to stay with our aunt and uncle Duvekot and their three grown-up children, on the outskirts of Goes. This was a far more modern and spacious house than the one we had been living in with my grandparents in the center of town. Even this house was not heated due to the lack of fuel. Only the kitchen was warm when my aunt Ella was cooking on the gas stove. With six kids in the house, my brother Bert and I had to a single bed in a very small guest room. There was no hot running water in the house and we shared a small cold water wash basin in our room. One mental image that has stuck with me all these years is of our two wash cloths draped over the side of the basin, frozen stiff when we got up in the morning. The window was completely frosted over on the inside. So this was Holland. We were grateful to be safe and to be given a temporary home, but it was a wrenching adjustment.

Because I was now 11 years old, they couldn't put me into second grade. So they started me in fifth grade. I was still struggling with my multiplication tables and long division and knew I was far behind the other kids. Even writing correct Dutch grammar was quite hard. Learning to concentrate on home work was a strange and difficult thing that I resisted. My emotions were in turmoil. I had a lot of catching up to do and found myself getting poor grades. School became a problem that would follow me for years.

Figure 20 The de Vries family, after arriving in Nederland. From left to right: Jack, Dad, Bert, Jan and Joan. Goes, Zeeland, 1946.

Chapter Ten

A DIFFICULT MERGER

During our first year in Nederland, my family was immediately pulled apart again because my father needed to work in The Hague (Den Haag), while Jan was in medical school in Leiden, and Bert, Joan and I were guests in Goes.

Of course we were fortunate that my father was earning any salary at all. Had he also died in the camps, the four de Vries children would have been entirely dependent on our aunts and uncles for everything—for food and housing and for some love and affection. We were all reeling from the loss of our mother and from the loss of our home. During our years in the camps, we had dreamed of returning to a more recognizable life in Batavia.

Wearing Three Hats

Because of Dad's professional background and personal contacts in the East Indies, he was now thrust into the turbulent relationship between Nederland and Indonesia. He had remained an official of the Netherlands East Indies government and was now also working for the Kingdom of the Netherlands. He lived in a hotel in The Hague at the expense of both the Dutch and the Dutch East Indies governments. Of course it was impossible to have any of us children living with him in this hotel, and we rarely saw him.

While busy with his government jobs, Dad also had successfully approached the University of Wageningen where he had earned his economic doctorate before the war. In early 1947 he was installed as a full professor lecturing in tropical agricultural economics. He led a hectic life, traveling by train between The Hague on the coast and Wageningen in the center of the country. He was working part-time for two governments and a university, wearing three hats. He was literally unable to care for his children.

This unstable situation could not last for long, and so my father resumed his courtship of Alexandrine (Lexie) Zweede, whom he had met on Java in Kamp 10 and again in Batavia. She remained reluctant, and he was warned by her family members to stay away from her. Alexandrine (ahlexahndreenah) was still in mourning and didn't want any man's attention.

But the reality was that she had no income and began to wish for a more normal family setting for her three kids, and that included finding a father for them. Dad persisted in his courtship and in 1947 Lexie cautiously agreed to what amounted to a trial marriage and family merger.

This Was All Wrong

In July of 1947, Bert and Lexie married in The Hague, and as I stood in the back of the church, I cried my eyes out.

This was all wrong. She was not my mother. With mounting alarm, I had seen my father shower his attentions on this lady in Batavia a year earlier. I had been quite upset when she repeatedly pushed him away. Why was he so interested in this strange lady? How could he?

Once we got to Nederland, I had thought that I would never see her again, but now she re-appeared, all dressed up and enthusiastic about my father. I didn't trust her new attitude toward Dad. It felt forced and fake. And I felt that he was betraying our lost mother. I was upset and protested that she wasn't right for us.

After the wedding, my father rented a house in The Hague and I had no choice but to submit to a new family regime run by Lex Zweede. As a boy of thirteen I had no power to resist. My father backed her at every turn. I resented them both and began to sulk more and more. The best I could do was to refuse to call her "mother" or anything similar. For a long time I called her "Tante Lex" (Aunt Lex). That did not sit well with her and certainly angered my father. I felt he was not my friend anymore. How could he turn away from me like this?

And so began the difficult merger of the four de Vries children and the three Zweede children, and their respective parents. As kids and teenagers, we did not know each other and ranged in age from Jan de Vries at nineteen and already in Medical School to Johan Zweede at seven. We had not chosen each other. I was thirteen and about to enter the turbulence of puberty. It was hard to suddenly have three new siblings.

Figure 21 It was hard to suddenly have new siblings, for all of us.

Turning to Friends

As is often the case, when kids are at odds with their parents at home, they turn to their friends. What we now call our "peer group" we just called "friends." So in The Hague I poured my energy into creating new friends. My classmates and I explored all sorts of games—some on the street, some at our homes, some in a nearby park. We rode our bikes all over our suburb of Scheveningen. We went skating in a nearby enclosed rink. In the summer we biked to the beach, where we often competed in gymnastics. In my own mind, I was turning away from the tensions and resentments at home, and looking for ways to feel better.

When I was promoted to seventh grade in a new school, I failed too many exams and was told I would have to repeat. My father decided to get me out of the house and so I lived on a dairy farm with a wonderful foster family for the rest of that school year.

In the fall of 1949 I was sent off to a boarding school in Zeist, near the center of the nation. That was a relief for me and no doubt for my parents. This private school for "difficult boys" was relatively small and set on a beautiful campus. I loved this new environment and made new friends easily. I was repeating the seventh grade, and for the first time in my life I began to get good grades in school, mostly because there was a supervised study hall after dinner every night.

That first Christmas of 1949, my friends were all excited about the prospect of going home. I dreaded going home. When Easter came around, it was the same situation, and I felt different from my friends because of it.

There were a few other boys who had also spent the war years in Japanese camps on Java. A particularly good friend was Jaap Besijn whose family had remained intact and now had a new luxurious house near Amsterdam. Jaap's father was a prominent business man and drove a brand new American car. That was quite a luxury in those days. Once the school year was over, I was invited to stay with his family. Their house in the North Sea dunes had a nearby tennis court and Jaap had already had some lessons. So I tried my hand at tennis, and one day his mother came out to the red clay courts with an Air Mail letter from my father. It brought major news. My Dad had been offered a position as a senior economist by the World Bank in Washington, DC, and we were going to America in the fall.

107

Moving to America

This was to prove another turning point in my life and the lives of everyone in my family. It was 1950, and the newspapers were filled with the carnage of war in Korea that summer. The North Koreans were driving the Americans into the small "Pusan Perimeter" and the daily headlines were horrifying. When he heard my news, my friend Jaap congratulated me and said I was lucky to be escaping the new war threatening Western Europe. Stalin had not disarmed at the end of the war, and his large tank armies were nearby on the East German border. There was ominous talk of a new World War.

Of course I felt excited and lucky. America was the land everyone admired. America had won the war. They had the most modern airplanes, the most streamlined cars, and their cities had skyscrapers. And we were going there to live.

The World Bank was, and still is, an agency of the United Nations. It paid for our travel to America on the *Nieuw Amsterdam*, the flagship of the Holland America Line. To our delight, we would be traveling first class with diplomatic visas on this luxury liner. As a result, in the fall of 1950, my step-mother Lex, her children Annelies and Johan, and my sister Joan and I set out from Rotterdam for New York. My father was already on a mission for the World Bank and my three older brothers were enrolled in their medical and engineering schools in Nederland—in Leiden and in Delft.

Figure 22 The merged de Vries/Zweede family in The Hague in 1950, just before most of us moved to Washington. Top row, from left to right: Bert de Vries, Bob Zweede, Lexie and Bert de Vries, Jan de Vries. Bottom row, left to right: Annelies Zweede, Jack de Vries, Johan Zweede, Joan de Vries.

This was one of the most exciting and wonderful experiences of my life up till then. The luxury was out of this world, especially in contrast to our modest life in Nederland and our war years in the Far East. The food was extravagant and the interior luxury of the ship was simply beautiful.

Naturally I was anxious to learn English as fast as I could. At my prep school, I had just begun my first English language classes. In those years in Holland, French was considered far more important, and I had already struggled with that grammar for some years. As a result, my English was primitive. In the movie theatre on board ship I enjoyed "Tea for Two," and remember paying close attention to the words. Yes, I could understand some of Doris Day's words, but not all.

Johan and I enjoyed our large first class cabin, but when the weather worsened in mid-ocean we got seasick. The steward brought us apples and crackers and told us we would get better if we ate only those two things. He was right. Nevertheless, we were all happy to see the Statue of Liberty as we slid into New York harbor. It was a great adventure for all of us.

Chapter Eleven

SETBACKS

Our first house in Washington, DC, was on Cathedral Avenue, near the Florham Park Hotel, the Washington Zoo and Rock Creek Park. In late October 1950, I had my 16th birthday right after we arrived. We were wide-eyed about all the details of living in a strange country. Just about everything was different from our life in Nederland. The houses, the cars, the supermarkets, the way people dressed, even the look of the coins and paper currency. Understanding and trying to speak a few basic English words was intimidating. The language was still a barrier for us, so we spoke mostly Dutch at home. I also realized that my Dutch nickname "Ko" would not be pronounced and accepted very well by Americans, and so I decided on "Jack" instead.

After we had unpacked, it was time to go to school again. I don't know why, but I was placed in the ninth grade, rather than the eighth. Perhaps it was because I was sixteen. This would become "Sink or Swim" with a vengeance. I did a little swimming and a lot of sinking.

English as a Second Language

At Alice Deal junior high school I struggled to understand the text books and strained to understand spoken English. People speaking a foreign language always appear to speak much too fast. Whenever the American adults and kids spoke to me, I found myself apprehensive and tense. Did I understand, and what should I try to say in reply? With hesitation, I would try out some short English sentences in my head and worry about the correct pronunciation.

During the day at school, the teachers had experience with foreign kids like me and were understanding and willing to repeat the instructions more slowly. Some of my new classmates also made an effort to explain things. That first year I did well in French and squeaked by in geometry. In the other subjects I couldn't really understand the textbooks and had difficulty with the exam questions.

On the home front it also became clear that I was once again living in a house controlled by my step-mother. I had been out of the house for most of the last two years, first on the dairy farm and then in the private school in Zeist. In the meantime I had probably matured a bit and was now more accepting of Lex Zweede. I believe she had also begun to adjust to the new reality.

While Bob, the oldest Zweede boy, had remained at the University of Delft in Holland, Annelies and Johan had moved into this American house with me and my sister Joan. Annelies was about four years older and Johan was six years younger than I was. I liked them both, and that made this adjustment process a bit easier.

"You Don't Know Baseball?"

While the school work was difficult, my worst set-back came because I couldn't play any of the American sports, although at 16 I was pretty tall and athletic-looking.

"You don't know baseball? Oh, let me show you—you just hit the ball and run around the bases. What about basketball or football?"

"No, in Holland we did gymnastics and played soccer and a bit of water polo. We didn't have all these large playing fields at school."

My poor English was not held against me, but not playing any American sports was unforgivable. In high school, during the winter we all had to play basketball indoors for gym class. I had never even tried to dribble and shoot one of these large balls. I was really ashamed of myself when the ball was stolen before I got close enough to try for the basket. When the time came for teams to be formed in gym, I was always called last—the leftover guy. That hurt, day in, day out

Not understanding the jokes told at the lunch tables also made me uneasy. In Holland I had been quite popular with the other boys, especially in my last year in boarding school. I was upset and really non-plussed that I was suddenly so unpopular. Here in Washington it was clear that I didn't measure up. I began to withdraw, and soon it was all too easy not to study at home, especially because I still remained quite at odds with my step-mother. As a result, I got very mediocre grades, which made me feel even more of an outcast and gave me even less encouragement to study.

That first year was the worst for me. My parents were trying out various churches and settled on a Congregational church near the Washington Cathedral. They decided it would be good for me to make friends with the teenage social church group. They signed me up and I thought perhaps I would make some friends.

It didn't work out too well. At one of their mixers, a very self-confident, pretty American girl came up to me. She was carrying a clip-board and said:

"So Jack, what is your pet peeve?"

"I don't know...... What?"

"You know, your <u>Pet Peeve!</u>"

"I don't know."

I still didn't understand and shook my head, becoming more and more embarrassed. Someone else probably explained what it was all about. I was so uncomfortable that I began to avoid going to this church group. I didn't want to have another fight about it with my parents, so I just pretended I was going there every Sunday afternoon. I'll never forget walking the neighborhood between the church and our house, for what seemed endless hours, and feeling ashamed. When I was quizzed at home I probably said yes, I was making new friends. Lying about it made me feel even worse.

In the summer of 1951, my older brother Bert and my step-brother Bob left Holland to join the rest of the family in Washington. They had finished their first year of engineering studies at Delft. This was a welcome addition, of course, but it also meant we had to move into a larger house. This second house was on Kanawha Street, much farther north and near the Chevy Chase circle. We all lived there for the next three years. I went to Woodrow Wilson high school, where I tried very hard to earn decent grades and tried even harder to make friends.

An Adventure in New Mexico

My high school years were not all doom and gloom. In the summer of 1952 I had a happy adventure. My older brothers Bert and Bob, and their college friend Claude, allowed me to go with them on a summer job. The Federal Bureau of Land Management hired us to help survey public lands in New Mexico and California for the entire summer.

We drove across the country in Claude's old car and saved money by avoiding the motels. On the first night, we all slept on picnic tables at a roadside rest stop outside Wheeling, West Virginia. On other nights we just pulled over and spread our sleeping bags on the ground. In Kansas, we drove long stretches of arrow-straight roads that would suddenly make a ninety degree turn. We found that we were driving along the boundary of somebody's farm. Incredible, compared to Holland. In spite of the blistering heat, and without air conditioning, we finally reached Albuquerque, where Bert and I were dropped off. Bob and Claude went on to northern California.

My brother and I became part of a small group of guys living in large tents in the open countryside near Farmington, New Mexico. There was no electricity or running water, and we drank from "air bags" that kept their contents cool through evaporation. Every Saturday the camp cook drove his truck into Farmington to buy groceries. That was a good break from the work week, and we rode into town with him. The laundromat was always the first stop.

The whole summer was an adventure in a landscape we had never seen before. These were huge stretches of un-inhabited arid terrain. There wasn't enough vegetation to keep any livestock.

We were told that some of the oil companies wanted to lease these empty mesa lands in order to drill for oil and natural gas. But first, the Federal Government had to have these public lands accurately surveyed. That is what we did. Led by a professional surveyor, we all learned on the job. We hiked all day to cut down tough old trees, so that we could physically measure the distances with a surveyor's steel "chain." This was a specialized, narrow steel tape-measure that we carried from post to post, mile after mile, up and down the mesas.

116

A Taste of Independence

I enjoyed being accepted as an adult by the other men in the crew. My English vocabulary and pronunciation were now much improved, and so I felt good about myself. Much better than I felt in high school where I just couldn't ever catch up in sports.

At some point during this summer in New Mexico, I think I became more and more enthusiastic about being in America, and perhaps even staying in America. My brothers also loved this wide open country with its hot weather. This was much more like the tropical Dutch East Indies we had grown up in. We knew that the Sukarno government was not allowing us to return to Java, and we didn't have much affection for Holland with its tight spaces and cold, rainy weather. Permanently staying in America became an attractive idea.

At the end of the summer Bert and I hitched a ride to Los Angeles and flew to San Francisco, where we hooked up with Bob and Claude for the drive back to Washington. We found snow in the Sierras, swam in the Great Salt Lake, visited the Mormon Temple and headed for many more days on the road, always sleeping on the ground near the car. The entire summer was a great adventure for us all.

There is probably no better way to appreciate the size of this country than by driving from coast to coast. In 1952, before there were any interstate highways, it took many days to cross the country on the old two-lane roads.

Looking back to that summer of 1952, I think I grew much closer to Bert de Vries and Bob Zweede. Bob now became a real brother in my mind. In time, Annelies and Johan Zweede also became real family.

No College for Me

Back in Washington I endured another two years of Wilson High. My school years had been one long downer. School had drained me of self-confidence, with far too many embarrassments and short-comings. That's why I refused to consider going to college, even though my brothers were all getting their university degrees and my father was an Economics Ph.D. at the head of his department at the World Bank.

Refusing to take the SAT exams or apply to any college confirmed my "Black Sheep" status at home, but I was defiant and angry. My step-mother told me that becoming a plumber or truck driver was a perfectly honorable course in life, if that's what I chose to do instead of college. My father had long since given up on me.

These high school years became an awful negative spiral for me. I was on my way to becoming a failure. I wanted to get out of my parents' house and away from any more studying, even though I had no real alternative in mind. I needed to be on my own. I wanted to be treated as an adult, as I had been on the surveying job in New Mexico.

Why Not Join the Air Force?

As luck would have it, one of our neighbors was an Air Force colonel at the Pentagon. He took a liking to me, and I admired him because he had flown jets in combat in the Korean War. Colonel Splain had said not everyone has to go to college right away, and if I didn't feel ready now, why not join the Air Force and maybe become a jet pilot. That appealed to me, and I volunteered for the Air Force. I took the day-long physical and mental tests at a nearby base, and all was well until the very end of the day. My papers revealed that I was still a subject of the Kingdom of the Netherlands, here on diplomatic visa.

The Air Force man told me I couldn't join because I had to become a US citizen first. The US Navy and Marine Corps had the same rule. After a meeting at the Dutch embassy, I learned that I could waive my draft exemption and put myself on a waiting list with the US Army.

The man at the embassy said: "Mr. de Vries, you will be a man without a country if you join the armed forces of any other nation, so think about this carefully." Then I also found out that there was a war-time law that said after ninety days in the US Army, foreign volunteers would qualify for naturalization, so I allowed myself to be drafted.

Colonel Splain said he was sorry my path into the Air Force was blocked and promised to do what he could to get me stationed in Europe once I had finished Basic Training. That infantry training in Georgia turned out to be a very cold shower of reality. The US Army knows how to

119

completely strip you of your previous personality and to turn you into an obedient soldier. I stuck it out, and after ninety days, indeed I became a naturalized US citizen.

At the age of 21, I was the first one in my family to become a US citizen, eventually followed by all of my siblings. I had wanted to be treated as an adult and to be on my own, and now I was.

Chapter Twelve

ON MY OWN IN THE ARMY

"Hey, de Vries! Company commander wants to see you. Right now." Just me? This is trouble. What have I done? I have no idea.

I walk to the company commander's office and report with my best salute. We are alone in his office, and he glares at me as he scans some papers.

"Who do you know at Third Army Headquarters, here in California?"

"Nobody, Sir."

"Well, I'll be G*d-damned ...... you're the only man on this entire base with orders for Paris, France. Now get the hell out of here."

"Yes, Sir."

The year was 1955 and the place was Fort Ord, California. I was a private in the US Army and now I had orders to fly to Paris. Unbelievable! So Colonel Splain had kept his word and pulled some strings at the Pentagon to get me stationed in Europe, after all.

Because I knew how to type, the Army had given me the job of clerk typist at the 12th Evacuation Hospital, outside Monterey, California. This was a MASH company, and I was the supply clerk for this mobile field hospital.

After finishing Basic Training in Georgia and South Carolina, I had been shipped across country to California by train. I learned to love weekend passes and trips to go body-surfing at Huntington Beach or hitch-hiking to Yosemite National Park with a buddy. From Carmel, we rented bikes to see the Seventeen Mile Drive along the ocean.

Now, by some miracle, I had orders to fly to Paris and report to an outfit called the 22d Transportation Company, supporting the NATO headquarters. This small company existed to provide the cars and drivers assigned to the highest-ranking Allied generals, admirals, and commanders at SHAPE, the Supreme Headquarters Allied Powers Europe.

My orders specified that I would first fly home to Washington, DC, and then on to Paris. Flying to the East Coast on TWA was far more enjoyable than the troop train had been, especially when the lovely stewardess addressed me as "Sir." In Basic Training nobody had ever called me anything except "Hey You!"

In Washington I called on Colonel Spain to thank him for getting me stationed in Paris. When it was time to leave, the flight was cancelled because the French airport workers were on strike. After a long wait, I was ordered to go by troop ship from Hoboken, NJ. This was in December of 1955, and the North Atlantic was in an uproar, so there was a lot of seasick misery in very cramped quarters.

At long last we docked in Bremerhaven. Most of the other men went to their assigned bases in West Germany. I was part of a small group that went to Paris by train. We were all quite excited as we were driven through the City of Light to NATO headquarters near Versailles.

American GI in Paris

When we had weekend passes, we could take the special green bus with the SHAPE emblem on its side into the city, where it dropped us off at the Étoile, by the Arc de Triomphe. So my buddies and I would have a cup of coffee on the Champs Elysée and watch the girls go by. We walked down to the Louvre quite a few times, and felt proud that we were looking at all these famous paintings without someone pushing us to do so. I even went to the Opéra and to the Opéra Comique. I was too much of a straight arrow to go to Place Pigalle with some of the other guys. My one evening at the famous Lido nightclub and its elegant topless dancers was as racy as it got for me.

This being 1956, we were twice restricted to the base in response to the tragic Hungarian Revolution and the Suez Crisis. President Eisenhower was suddenly denounced by the French and British governments because he forbade American assistance in the Anglo-French seizure of the Canal. Meanwhile, the walls in Paris were full of slogans proclaiming that Algeria was actually a French province and therefore should never be given independence: "Algérie Française".

In my squad room at SHAPE, near Versailles, the fellow in the adjoining bunk was John Doty, who came from Evanston, Illinois, and had two years of college under his belt. John was also a clerk typist, in charge of ordering the supplies for the motor pool. He began taking courses at night at a nearby Army base, sponsored by the University of Maryland. We were good friends and he kept after me to take some university extension courses too.

Reshaping my Own Future

To voluntarily take any kind of schooling was quite abnormal for me, to say the least. But nobody in my family would know if I once again got a bad grade. I was so bored with Army life that finally I also took a course at Camp des Loges—always in the evening, hitching a ride with a colonel who was adding credits toward his graduate degree. My course was about the causes of the Civil War. I liked this course and liked the young instructor. The ideas were interesting, so I worked hard and did well. When the grades came in, I got an A minus. Holy Toledo! This was a small class and we were all adults, working because we wanted to. So I took the next course and got another A.

By now my two-year Army hitch was nearing an end, and I was urged to re-enlist. I was turned off by the rules and routines of Army life and saw that it would be a dead end. Now what? What else could I do? Maybe I really need to have more skills. I am interested to learn more about how the world works, and I do want to get ahead in life—

away from the lack of respect I'm receiving as an Army private, always having to do what I am told.

Maybe I should try to get into a college after I'm discharged, but I know I'm a bad student, always just getting by with C's and D's and being an outcast. School had brought humiliation and shame, year after year.

Well, I have to try, and here in the Army, I have done well. At six foot two and 165 pounds I'm in good shape. My English is nearly perfect now. When I came into Basic Training in Georgia I was just as good as any other guy— or just as bad—at learning how to march and shoot a rifle, and learning all the new rules of Army life, for that matter.

Figure 23 Pfc. Jack de Vries, US Army, SHAPE, France, 1956.

Chapter Thirteen

CHRISTMAS AT THE PALACE

While I was at SHAPE during the summer of 1956, my Dad was asked to return to Holland to become the president of a new graduate school focused on economic development in the Third World.

For Christmas I got a pass and took the train from Paris to The Hague. My father and step-mother were living in the former royal palace there. It was the oldest of the royal palaces, begun in 1591, and the city had grown up around it, so it was downtown now. A fire in the central ballroom had caused Queen Juliana and her court to move to other palaces. Even after the center of this very large palace complex had acquired a temporary new roof, historic Paleis Noordeinde had remained mostly empty.

In 1955, the Universities of the Netherlands had gotten together to discuss how best to help train the future leaders of Asia, Africa and Latin America. They wanted to create a graduate school, but none of the universities had space for such an Institute of Social Studies. Luckily this board's honorary chairperson was none other than Queen Juliana. She offered the use of the old palace in downtown The Hague as the first home for this graduate school that would concentrate on economic development, regional planning and governance. My father, Professor Bert de Vries, was on the board of this Netherlands Universities Foundation for

International Cooperation (NUFFIC). Because of his expertise in economic development in the tropics, he was recruited as its founding president. He left the World Bank in Washington, DC, and moved back to Holland in the summer of 1956. Dad would remain as the Institute's first president for the next ten years until he retired at age 65. Not too many people can say they lived in a royal palace for ten years.

Because my younger step-brother, Johan Zweede, was only 16, my parents brought him to The Hague to continue his high school education. I shared his bedroom at the palace when I visited. Our parents had moved into the so-called "bronze quarter," the entire left wing of the palace, where Queen Juliana herself was born. The enormous size of the rooms, the huge windows, the damask-covered walls, the chandeliers and the height of the ceilings—it was all quite...um... palatial.

Over dinner that Christmas, my Dad said, "Well Jack, I think you said you will be discharged from the Army in February, is that right? What are your plans for the future?" Time to eat some humble pie. I braced myself and said, "I don't want to stay in the Army, so I've decided to try for college." There, I've actually come out and said it. He seemed to approve, but cautiously. Everyone knew Jack was not a good student.

"Do you know what kind of college would be best for me Dad?"

"No, I don't really know much about the American university system. And also Jack, as you know, I'm earning

Dutch guilders now, and the currency restrictions make it extremely difficult for me to buy US dollars. So I won't be able to help pay for your tuition." Not an encouraging start for my new course in life.

Figure 24 Lexie and Bert with Johan, living at "Paleis Noordeinde."

The next evening Dad came to dinner and told me that two gentlemen had just arrived at the Institute, and one is the Dean of Education at the University of Delaware. "Why don't you talk with Bill Penrose about American colleges and perhaps get some advice on which ones to aim for?"

Bill Penrose Opens a Door

I walked down the palace halls and found Mr. Penrose and told him my idea of doing a 180 degree turn and trying for college after all. He told me I could use his name and apply to the University of Delaware. He asked if I qualified for the GI Bill, and I explained that I just missed it. The country had to be at war while you served in the armed forces, and combat in Korea had ended before I joined the Army.

So what about a scholarship? Did I have any chance, with my poor high school record? Lord only knows what Dean Penrose must have thought! He took me seriously and told me that he knew a gentleman in Wilmington, Delaware, who might help me in my search for a scholarship. His name was W. W. Laird, and this was his address.

So as soon as I got back to my supply clerk office at SHAPE, I typed a letter to this Mr. Laird, mentioned having met Dean Penrose, and explained my hope of going to college. (I have saved the onion skin carbon copy of this historic letter.)

In due time I was honorably discharged and was invited to stay with my step-sister Annelies and her husband Alfred Walton, who were recently married and living in Brooklyn. So I wrote Mr. Laird and took the train to Wilmington and had my interview at the University of Delaware. The man there looked at my high school record and allowed as how they rarely took anyone with such poor grades. Oh boy, here comes the embarrassment again, but I just have to fight my way through it.

Chapter Fourteen

A VOTE OF CONFIDENCE

My next stop was far more encouraging. I met Mr. Laird in his Wilmington office and told him my story of arriving in Holland at age 11, after the War, with a faint memory of first grade in Batavia, in what was then the Netherlands East Indies, and now Indonesia. The Japanese did not allow school in the concentration camps, and so we were all about three years behind by the time we were evacuated to Nederland in 1946. I talked about my mother starving to death in the camps and my difficult time with my step-mother after the War in Holland. They had put me in the fifth grade where of course I had a hard time, but at least I spoke Dutch and could read the books. After moving from one school to another in Holland, flunking out, and repeating in seventh grade, I had finally begun to hit my stride in 1949-1950 in my boarding school, earning good grades and also being popular with my classmates there.

Then came the move to Washington and falling flat on my face in the American high school. My vow never to go to college, my positive Army experience in Paris and my astonishing grades when I ventured to take those college courses at night. I explained about my father being in The Hague and earning guilders, and my search for a scholarship.

This kind gentleman listened quietly and asked: "Have you saved any money for college?" "Yes, Sir, I've saved more than half of my Army pay. And I will be working this spring and summer to save more. But I don't know how much more I will need because I don't know what college I can get into. What kind of college do you think I should aim for?"

"I'm not going to recommend any specific school Jack—that is up to you. I do think you should accept the best college that admits you. And once you have made that decision, let me know how much money you will need to go there, and my scholarship foundation may be able to make up the difference."

Did I hear that right? Here was this perfect stranger who was giving me one hell of a vote of confidence, while my father was barely lukewarm about me and my belated try at a college.

When I got back to Annelies and Alfred, I was beginning to think that maybe a small but good college such as Tufts might be the best place to aim for. Alfred had been Phi Beta Kappa at Yale and gone on to the Harvard Law School and was now an attorney at AT&T.

He said: "You're a bright guy, Jack. I really enjoyed my college years, and I'm sure you will too. I'm sending for application forms for Yale and Harvard. I thought Cambridge and Boston had a lot more to offer than New Haven, but you'll be happy on either campus."

I was mortified and protested that they would laugh in my face. Nevertheless, I finished the Yale application and the one for Tufts. The people in New Haven did not laugh at me. They said that if they were to admit me, they would also give me a small scholarship. They said they had very good experiences with veterans because they were highly motivated to make up for lost time. That was a confidence booster because it certainly described me. I thought Yale would be much too difficult for me, so I pinned my hopes on Tufts.

I took the train to Boston, stayed in the YMCA and took the streetcar to Tufts in Medford. On the way there, I was surprised to see that the streetcar passed under Harvard Square and I thought that on the way back I would get rid of the incomplete Harvard application........if Yale was too hard, Harvard was out of the question!

The admissions guy at Tufts was taken aback by my poor grades, but polite, and so I hoped against hope. Maybe, maybe, they might take me.

I Shouldn't Even Be Here

On the way back, I got off the streetcar at Harvard Square, found the University Hall and handed my incomplete application to the secretary. She said, "But you don't have an appointment here." I said, "Yes, I just wanted to drop this off, and I shouldn't even be here." She asked me to take a seat—it was lunch time and very few were in the office. After a few minutes, out came a tall, white-haired gentleman who said something along the lines of "Well, you're here without an appointment, but I can give you a few minutes." I sat bolt upright, expecting the worst, but this gentleman scanned my file, leaned back and lit his pipe. Then he said, "Well, Jack, you seem to have an unusual background. Tell me about yourself."

No comments about my poor school record....so I began to explain about my very sketchy education, beginning on Java, the lack of school during the war, the hopscotch years in Holland and then not speaking English when I arrived in Washington. How in my first year I had been able to get decent grades only in geometry and French because I couldn't really read the textbooks for the other courses. How I had hated high school and how I wound up in the Army, gingerly daring to take some courses at night and finding that I liked reading and even studying, once it was my own idea.

I found out later that this gentleman was Eric Cutler, the Dean of Admissions for Harvard. He asked if I had taken the SAT exam. No, I had not. Did I know how I scored on the Armed Forces IQ test? Yes, I was told it was pretty good. Well, he said, "We can fill the freshman class with straight A students if that is what we wanted, but we like to have more variety, and sometimes the Admissions Committee will consider a diamond in the rough. If you think you can do the work here, why don't you finish the application, take the SAT test and try again."

Diamond in the Rough?

I clearly remember walking down the granite steps of University Hall and feeling myself blush with astonishment and exhilaration. He didn't dismiss me, and said they might actually consider me.......But could I do the work here? I had the worst possible study habits. I had none.

After a few weeks, I moved in with my step-brother Bob Zweede who lived in Cleveland. He was engaged to a lovely girl whom he had met in high school in Holland after the war. Jeannette van Zanen had also been through the Japanese camps. In her case, she and her family were imprisoned on Sumatra where her mother died of starvation. The story of her camp has been well told in the book *Song of Survival* and the movie based on it, called "Paradise Road," starring Glenn Close (see the bibliography). In time Bob and Jeannette were married and are now retired in Sonora, California.

Bob had heard that the iron ore freighters were about to swing back into service as the ice was melting on the Great Lakes. These 200-yard-long ships carried iron ore from the Mesabi Range on Lake Superior to South Chicago, Gary, Indiana, and sometimes Cleveland. So after taking the SAT tests and completing my Harvard application, I became a deckhand, working for US Steel. They gave you a bunk and fed you, so what you earned you kept. There were three deckhands on board and we were treated as dumb animals by the cursing bosun. I came on board in my Army boots with my Army duffel bag over my shoulder and was so determined that I took all the cr*p he dished out for the next 16 long and lonely weeks.

We got our mail at the Sault Ste. Marie locks between Lake Superior and Lakes Michigan or Huron. I lived for the affectionate letters from Babs Beasley, whom I had met during my University of Maryland classes and who had become my first real girlfriend. I learned French kissing in Paris......not bad.

The Phone Booth at the Steel Mill

Finally, one hot muggy night, we were tied up at the US Steel blast furnace in Gary, Indiana, unloading iron ore. I got permission to go ashore and found a phone booth. I called Bob in Cleveland to ask if any colleges had replied to my applications yet.

I remember it as if it was yesterday, because he said: "Yes, you got some answers. Do you want to go to Harvard or Yale? You also got in at Delaware and Tufts."

Woohoo! as they would say today. I asked Bob to send a telegram to Mr. Laird saying I would like to go to Harvard if he could make up the difference between my savings and the $1200 in tuition, room and board. Yes, in 1957, it was $1200. I still have the papers. He sent congratulations and suggested I come see him before going to Cambridge in the fall.

Steep Rock Face

I was thrilled and scared at the same time. Could I possibly scale this steep rock face called Harvard? Well, they were giving me a chance, and by God, I was going to give it my all. So I wrote to my parents in The Hague with my incredible news. In time there was a letter from my step-mother Lexie, saying that she and my Dad were quite concerned about this and that it was a mistake to try for Harvard. I should try for a small college that was not going to be so difficult. I was incredulous, angry and defiant. I tried to re-assure myself with the vote of confidence from Mr. Laird and the encouragement from my brother-in-law Alfred Walton. I was going to tackle Harvard, run like hell to catch up, and leave the doubters far behind.

After coming ashore from my ore boat, I took the train to see Mr. Laird in Wilmington. He congratulated me and told me my scholarship would also include some money from his "Screwball Fund." He said it was important at my stage in life to have some extra money to explore unusual things. In due time I learned to ski in New Hampshire and Vermont, bought tickets to the Boston Symphony, and added some necessary new clothes. In the 1950's at Harvard, we were not allowed into the dining rooms without a coat and tie.

Running to Catch Up

One month after my freshman registration I had my 23rd birthday, and found myself surrounded by mostly 18-year-old boys. They had been very well-prepared at Exeter, Andover, Choate, New Trier and other top schools around the country. I did not fit in with them, and I felt like an outsider.

Figure 25 Lowell House. Harvard College. Cambridge, MA.

When the grades came in, it was once again very discouraging for me. Of course I was scared and tried and tried again to learn to concentrate on the assigned reading and to write the term papers. It had been three years since high school and my self-discipline was close to zero when it came to studying.

One incident has stayed with me all these years. As freshmen we were all required to take an English literature course, and so we read Yeats and analyzed poetry, and it was all Greek to me. I got D's and C's. My section leader in the English literature course was Professor Brower, who was also the head of the entire English Department. Knowing that I was failing, I waited for him after class and explained that I didn't know how to do what was expected. I think he sensed that I was not lazy, and he also noticed the military overcoat I was wearing. He asked if I was a veteran and how long I had been out of school. "Why don't you come to my home this Sunday afternoon, and perhaps I can give you some advice?" he said. We sat in his living room, and he explained that I had to cite phrases in the text in order to justify my interpretations and opinions about what Yates or Frost had meant to say. I think that incident has always stayed with me because it said to me that Harvard cared about individual students, provided they were really trying. After nearly failing in the fall, I got a B for the course and even got a sentence of congratulations on my final exam from Professor Brower.

Once I realized I had a chance of graduating with a degree in liberal arts, I made an appointment with the Dean of Admissions at the Harvard Graduate School of Business Administration, across the river. "I have just finished my freshman year at the College here and want to prepare for the Business School. I've taken an Economics course, but don't know what other courses will prepare me best. What courses would you recommend?"

Dean Chafee said, "Mr. de Vries, you know there is no such thing as a 'business major' at Harvard College. Here at the Business School we have admitted people who had majored in English, Music or even Sanskrit at college. We admitted them only because they had earned very high grades in those fields. The important thing is for you to catch fire in whatever field you choose. Really catch fire and excel." I've never forgotten that amazing viewpoint.

My Brandywine Summers

As the end of my freshman year approached, I began looking for a summer job. Mr. Laird suggested that I work for the Brandywine Valley Association (BVA), and I was happy to do so.

The Brandywine River had always been important to Mr. Laird's hometown of Wilmington, Delaware. The river had provided the water power for the original Du Pont Company gun powder mills in the eighteenth century. He had grown up in this valley and loved its beauty and history. The Brandywine bordered his Wilmington property as well as his cattle ranch across the border near West Chester, PA. Mr. Laird and his likeminded friends had formed this organization in an effort to reduce the silt and industrial pollution that was choking the river. Most of that pollution originated upriver, across the border, in Pennsylvania.

I was happy to work for the Brandywine Valley Association for each of my college summers.

Working quietly behind the scenes as financier and philanthropist, Mr. Laird was an important benefactor for the University of Delaware, the Tatnall School, the Hagley Museum, and the Gilbert & Sullivan players at Longwood Gardens, as well as countless other civic organizations such as the BVA.

Figure 26 My beloved mentor, Mr. W. W. Laird.

Honors Tutorial

By my junior year, I qualified for the Honors Program, which meant I was in the top ten percent in my grades. I was concentrating in Government and now qualified for Honors Tutorial. It was quite stimulating to be taking Government courses with Kissinger and Brezinsky, Economics with Galbraith, and Social Studies with David ("Lonely Crowd") Riesman. But the need to study in the evenings after dinner had been really difficult for me. I vividly remember trudging from Lowell House to Lamont library, night after night, pushing myself to really concentrate because I couldn't let Mr. Laird down. I would be so embarrassed if my Harvard grades were mediocre. I might even lose my scholarship and would certainly lose my newfound self-confidence.

Figure 27 Jack de Vries, Harvard College, 1960.

Instead, after nearly flunking out and running to catch up, I saw that I could succeed after all. My senior honors thesis was about the unique role of voluntary citizens associations in American Government, and a case study of the Brandywine Valley Association in particular.

In its efforts to improve the environment, the BVA was far ahead of its time. It brought leading citizens in the States of Delaware and Pennsylvania together in an effort to educate local political representatives about the need to combat the severe industrial pollution of the upper Brandywine River in Pennsylvania. Paper mills and steel mills were dumping chemicals into the river. Large fish kills had become all too common, and there were photos of paint peeling off the canoes near Wilmington. There were concerns that the quality of Wilmington's water supply was threatened.

The Brandywine originates in Pennsylvania and flows across the boundary into Delaware with blissful disregard for the political consequences. Neither state's government had been concerned enough to take remedial action. They had not cooperated on a regional basis until the private Brandywine Valley Association had made a convincing case and brought pressure to bear. We also persuaded the State of Pennsylvania to build flood control and water supply reservoirs on the upper reaches of the Brandywine, and I called on the various land owners to obtain the necessary easements for those successful dam projects.

Voluntary citizen associations are an American specialty. Few other nations have fostered such civic participation. In American government, whether at the local, state or federal level, voluntary associations play a fundamental role

Chapter Fifteen

PRACTICALLY ADOPTED

My special relationship with Mr. Laird and his family was formed and strengthened during each of the three college summers that I worked and lived in the Brandywine Valley. I was often invited for the weekend by the Laird family after they moved from "Louviers," their historic du Pont family home in Wilmington, to their large farm near West Chester, PA, for the summer season. In time, the Lairds became "family" for me, and I felt very privileged and happy. Their entire family embraced me warmly, and that felt just wonderful.

During these Harvard College years my self-confidence began to grow, and the new friends I was making made me feel good for the first time since those dark years in Washington. At Lowell House (Fig. 25), my roommates Ward Smith and Dan Phillips made me welcome. I soon enlarged my circle of close friends to include Rudy Ruggles, Bob Bray and Eustis Walcott. And now I had enough self-confidence to seek and find a number of girlfriends.

In one of his letters, Chick Laird said that he and Winnie Laird were happy to be my *in loco parentis*, and that is exactly what they became with each passing year. I soaked up their family affection and it made me stronger.

More Catching Up

In 1961, I graduated *cum laude* from Harvard College and was accepted by the Harvard University Graduate School of Business Administration, across the Charles River from Cambridge. Mr. Laird insisted I should have at least one year of business experience before starting with the Business School. That was excellent advice, and I worked as a financial statistician in Wilmington for the year between college and graduate school.

In retrospect, it seems that I was certainly breaking with my family's tradition of avoiding the world of business. Perhaps I was adopting Mr. Laird's viewpoints gained from his experience in the business world. He was the grandson of Pierre S. du Pont and was on the Board of the Du Pont Company.

Figure 28 The Harvard Business School, from across the Charles River.

My years at the Harvard Business School were once again difficult, academically. The famous "case method" of teaching emphasized the quantification of problems, and I found that my math skills were still shaky. Why was that? Didn't I have a normal education in arithmetic and algebra, like everyone else? Well, no. I realized that by the time I had graduated from the 12th grade in Washington in 1954, I had been in classrooms for only 8 years. I had never been in second, third and fourth grade because of the camps. In arithmetic your skills depend on what you learned the previous year. Not having those foundation years made all future math difficult. Then in Holland I had muddled through the fifth, sixth and seventh grade. Moving to the States at age 16, I skipped eighth grade, and started shakily with the ninth grade in Washington. At the "B School" we did not yet have any electronic calculators and I struggled with a slide rule. So the Harvard Business School was another difficult marathon for me, but I made it.

As my HBS graduation neared, I heard about the pre-eminent management consulting firm of McKinsey & Co. Partly because they were about to open an office in Amsterdam, they hired me in 1964, and I moved to Manhattan for training. To work for McKinsey was the ultimate opportunity for anyone graduating from the Harvard Business School. More students interviewed for McKinsey positions than with any other company that year. It was another pressure-cooker environment, but now I was in the real world of business, with important problems to be solved, and I learned a great deal.

149

In time, I moved to Wall Street as a research analyst with Baker Weeks & Co., which in turn led to a career in mergers and acquisitions at Wm. Sword & Co. and Morris Capital, Inc.

Figure 29 Jack de Vries, McKinsey & Co. New York, NY, 1964.

Not Without Help

I had been running to catch up for many years. I had come a long way from being the high school outcast and Army private, when my life was in an awful tailspin—but only because a number of people had given me a vote of confidence and support.

My brother-in-law Alfred Walton had encouraged me to apply to Yale and Harvard. All of the others who opened important doors were total strangers when I first met them, starting with Colonel Splain in Washington, John Doty at SHAPE, Dean Penrose in The Hague, and Eric Cutler and Professor Brower at Harvard.

By far the most important of these men was my *in loco parentis* Chick Laird in Wilmington, Delaware. He had also been a complete stranger when we first met and over the years had grown to become the father I wished for. I will always be grateful for his generosity, practical advice and true affection.

In retrospect, the two years in the US Army also proved to be a major turning point in my life. The Army sobered me up. It gave me a fierce determination to make up for lost time and to make a life of my own choosing.

I must admit that in my first year at Harvard I didn't enjoy the process of learning. The work was simply too difficult. In the next three college years, I discovered my own curiosity about how things fit together in the world, and I began to enjoy all the new thoughts and ideas that were spread out before me. Now I was doing it for my own reasons, and I wanted to learn more. Those night courses I had taken in the Army showed me that I could enjoy new insights, and that "Really Catching Fire to Excel" could lead to happier times.

Epilogue

Looking back over the years since 1947 when my father married Mrs. Zweede, it is clear that the difficult merger of their families became a success. Bert and Lexie grew to truly love each other over the years, and my Zweede/de Vries brothers and sisters certainly grew to love each other also. It is clear that each one of us had been under a lot of stress during and after the Japanese camps, and that I was a defiant young man headed for more disappointments. After suffering their own traumatic losses and even wishing to end their lives, Bert and Lexie did the best they could to help us rebuild our lives.

In retrospect, it is fortunate that our family merger succeeded. As with many families in our mobile society, we settled in different parts of the United States, and of course that limits regular face to face contact and closeness. Even though geography separated us, we have worked to stay in touch and have all supported each other, especially when that was most needed.

Chick and Winnie Laird, as well as Bert and Lexie de Vries, passed away some years ago, while my dear sister Joan de Vries Covey passed away more recently in San Mateo, CA at the age of 81. Her famous daughter, Joy Covey, died in 2013 in a traffic accident near her home in Woodside, CA. Joy had been the first Chief Financial Officer of Amazon.com and had successfully taken that company public.

Figure 30 My daughter Margot Kenaston's family visits us on Kauai in 2014. From left to right: Sydney, Margot, Matt and Charlie Kenaston with Jack de Vries and Vera Graye.

As of the time of this writing, now 70 years after the end of World War II, my remaining siblings and their children and grandchildren all live in the United States, scattered far and wide over at least eight states. Annie Zweede lives in Paris, while her father Johan Zweede lives in Fortaleza, Brazil. Ours is a well-traveled and well-educated clan.

My daughter Margot and her husband Matt Kenaston live in San Francisco with their daughters Charlotte and Sydney. After living in Manhattan from 1964 until 1972 and settling in Morristown, New Jersey, from 1972 until 2006, I retired to Fearrington Village, near Chapel Hill, North Carolina.

Jack de Vries, 2015

Acknowledgements

A number of friends here in Fearrington Village have encouraged me to tell my war-time stories, in front of small groups as well as in print.

My special thanks go to Ken Samuelson, who added my oral history to his large collection and invited me to tell my story to the Fearrington Veterans Club. The members of the Fearrington Writers' Group encouraged me to press on and introduced me to other authors who had successfully published. Laura Jenkins provided valuable editorial advice for this memoir.

I am especially indebted to my editor, Julia Hardy, who also formatted this entire book to the exacting specifications required by CreateSpace. My special thanks go to Paulette Webb who designed the cover of this book and assisted me with the illustrations.

I am grateful to Sharen Faye, who created the maps in this book, and to Vera Graye, Martha Ann Rabon and Katie Baer, who critiqued my early drafts.

This personal memoir is illustrated with selected maps, drawings and photos. Those illustrations not belonging to the author are in the public domain with a few exceptions; those appear courtesy of the artists or their families, who retain all rights: M. G. Hartley, *Mijn Kamp, maar niet door Hitler*, 1947, Amsterdam, and D. H. Volz in *De Japanse Burgerkampen*, 1963, Franeker, by Dr. D. van Velden.

Appendix One

Timeline of Major Events

1934   Jacobus E. de Vries born in Batavia; nicknamed "Ko" and later changed to "Jack."

1938   Our family furloughed to the Netherlands (Holland).

1940   Germany conquers Western Europe, including Holland.

1941   Japan attacks Pearl Harbor. The USA, Britain and the Netherlands East Indies declare war on Japan.

1942   Japan conquers our country. Dad remains at his civil service office in Bandoeng and begins secret resistance.

1943   The de Vries family interned in the "Bloemen Kamp" in Bandoeng, West Java.

1944   Dad arrested by the Secret Police in March. In October, the Americans land in the Philippines, north of us. In November,

Mom, Joan and Jack are moved to Central Java and into Banjoe Biroe Kamp 10 prison.

1945   Jack sent to concentration camp in Ambarawa. In April, Mom dies of starvation in Kamp 10 at age 47. Joan is 12 years old and only one in the family who knows.

In August, Hiroshima and Nagasaki are destroyed by the atom bombs and Japan surrenders. Sukarno declares an independent Republic of Indonesia.

In October, Dad finds Joan and Jack in Kamp 10 and they take a train to Bandoeng to join Jan and Bert. Gurkha advance units protect the camp from attack by fanatic natives.

1946   In early 1946, Dad and Jack are airlifted to Batavia. In April, Dad, Bert, Joan and Jack are evacuated to Holland. Jan remains to take final exams and joins us later that year to start Medical School in Leiden.

Dad earns salary as Professor at his alma mater in Wageningen and begins to court

Lexie Zweede. Jack, Bert and Joan live with a loving aunt and uncle in Goes, and resume their education.

1947   Dad marries Lexie Zweede. The two families merge and move to The Hague.

1950   Dad is recruited by the World Bank in Washington, DC. The merged de Vries/Zweede family joins him there. Culture shock requires many adjustments.

1955   Jack joins the US Army in February; he is stationed in California and Paris, France.

1956   Christmas at the Palace in The Hague where Jack meets Dean Penrose.

1957   Jack discharged from US Army. Meets Mr. Laird and works on ore boats. Receives scholarship and is admitted to Harvard College.

1961   Jack graduates from Harvard with honors.

1964   Jack graduates from the Harvard Business School, and joins McKinsey & Co. in New York.

Appendix Two

The Islands of Indonesia

Rather than interrupting the flow of the narrative with additional background information or foot-notes, I have included some historical perspectives here.

Today, Indonesia is home to about 250 million people and has the largest Muslim population in the world. It is spread over some 3,000 miles straddling the equator, between the Asian mainland and Australia. The Indonesian archipelago consists of about 13,000 islands, with thousands of dormant and active volcanoes. Super-imposed on the continental United States, Indonesia would spread from San Diego to Bermuda.

The East Indies have long been famous for their spices, such as pepper, mace, nutmeg and cloves. These were what Columbus was searching for in 1492, as well as the riches of China.

During the 1500's the Portuguese, the English and the Dutch mounted expeditions to these Spice Islands to establish a lucrative trade. In 1602, a group of powerful Dutch merchants founded the United East India Company or, by its Dutch initials, the VOC. This famous company also built a strong trading network with China, Japan, India and Ceylon. In time, the Dutch government was asked to protect these settlers and their outposts from other

European nations and native attacks. The East Indies became a Dutch colony in the beginning of the nineteenth century. Initially all trade with Europe was by sailing vessels, rounding the Cape of Good Hope.

During the early twentieth century, the Dutch East Indies became a rich source of plantation crops, most of which were exported to the world. Before oil was discovered by the predecessor of Royal Dutch Shell, tropical agriculture was by far the most important part of the economy. Eighty percent of the population was working in agriculture, both peasant and plantation agriculture. My father was an economist who specialized in tropical agricultural economics, working in the Ministry of Economic Affairs in Batavia.

The major crops were rice, sugar, rubber, coffee, tea and tobacco. The coffee must have appealed to many people, because a "cup of Java" still means coffee to most Americans.

Quinine grew well in the mountains of Java and became an important medicine to combat malaria throughout the tropics. Before the war, the Dutch controlled some 95% of the world's quinine production, called "kina" in those years. In British India, people took their bitter quinine with tonic and created the drink we all know as Gin and Tonic. Once the Japanese had conquered the Dutch East Indies, they not only obtained the supply of oil they so desperately wanted, but they also found a rich supply of rubber, tin and quinine. This meant that the British and American armed forces were suddenly faced with the loss of their anti-malarial protection, just as hundreds of thousands troops were being mobilized to fight in the jungles of the Pacific Islands and the mainland of Asia. Just in time, the American laboratories were able to produce *Atabrine* as a substitute. It turns your skin yellow, as if you have jaundice, and we saw it on the British and Australian soldiers at the end of the war.

Java is the most heavily populated island in Indonesia, and has historically been the center of culture and power. A great mountain range with many active volcanoes runs along the island's length. Mount Semeru, the highest peak, rises 12,000 feet above sea level. The island is about 700 miles long and from 60 to 130 miles wide. Java has several important seaports, and major cities are linked by road, rail and air. Every piece of land fit for cultivation is intensively farmed. Rice is grown on terraced hillsides.

Hindu traders came to Java after the first century A.D. and established powerful kingdoms. The largest Hindu temple in the world, the famous Borobudur, is situated in central Java, in the sultanate of Djogjakarta. By about 1500, the islanders were converted to Islam, although Bali remained Hindu.

In 1619 the Dutch founded Batavia (now Jakarta) and gradually spread their rule over Java, and eventually all the islands.

Because the Indonesian archipelago is spread over thousands of islands, some 700 different languages evolved in isolation. Before the war, my parents learned Sundanese, while the Zweedes spoke Javanese, although they lived on the same island. Today the national language of Bahasa Indonesia serves as a uniting force throughout the many islands.

When the Japanese invaded the Dutch East Indies in February of 1942, there were about 140,000 Dutch men, women and children living in the entire archipelago. Another 160,000 Dutch Eurasians were also classified as citizens of the Kingdom of the Netherlands. Most of the Dutch Eurasians were not interned. With a total population of the Dutch East Indies estimated at 68 million at that time, the Dutch were a very small minority.

During the War, about 20% of all our POW's died as slave laborers in Burma or Japan, and on the infamous "hell ships" that transported Allied soldiers to Japan. According to Dr. van Velden's authoritative book, the camps of Dutch women and children witnessed death rates ranging from 5% to 35% depending upon the camp's location. In Dad's Tjipinang jail the casualty rate is estimated at about 50%, reaching as high as 70% in some months.

In retrospect, it is tragic that the governments of Indonesia and the Netherlands were unable to stop the bloodshed and negotiate a peaceful and gradual transfer of power after the Japanese surrender in 1945.

The peace negotiations were led by Dr. van Mook. As acting Governor General of the Netherlands East Indies in Batavia, van Mook was caught up in the nearly impossible situation of dealing with the Dutch Government in The Hague, the British military and the Indonesian nationalists.

Every time van Mook painstakingly negotiated a tentative agreement with the Indonesians, his uninformed and rigid superiors in Holland overruled him. Peace negotiations were held with the Indonesians outlining a ten year transition period, but agreements were soon broken. Undisciplined gangs continued to attack the British and Dutch military in spite of cease fire agreements.

Eventually, the United Nations forced Holland to abandon the military operations aimed at enforcing the agreements negotiated with the Indonesians. Australia and the USA were particularly opposed to the return of colonial rule in the Netherlands East Indies.

Today, the Republic of Indonesia consists of all of the islands of the former Netherlands East Indies, eventually including the eastern half of New Guinea. In 1949, Indonesia gained full sovereignty.

Appendix Three

The Walled Prison Where My Mother Died

Figure 31 The Banjoe Biroe Camps, 11 and 10 (left to right), near Ambarawa. Photographed on January 28, 1945 by the crew of Major van Breemen's B-25 bomber.

The Leaflet Drops for the Camps on Java

The Airplane: B-25 Bomber, stationed in Northern Australia.

Sunset Over Java

The Crew: Six airmen of the Royal Dutch Air Force, led by Mayor F. van Breemen.

The Flight of 28 January, 1945:

"We began our flight at Potshot (Australia) and planned to return to Broome. To reach Soerabaja and Central Java and return would require a flight of 2,250 miles. We had planned to fly on 31 December 1944, but General van Oyen ruled out that date, believing it unsuitable for psychological reasons. So van Bremen's propaganda flight was scheduled for 28 January 1945.

"Just after midnight, we started plane number N 185, which was loaded with 32,000 pounds. When we sighted the island of Java, near Kediri, we encountered a broad weather front and had to climb to ten thousand feet. Just west of the Lawoe volcano, we entered the airspace over Java. Because of this detour, it was already daylight by the time we approached Soerabaja and our aircraft twice came under anti-aircraft fire. Although well-aimed, the stream of bullets did not hit our plane. By evasive action and by flying very low, our commander van Breemen was able to save our hides. After we dumped some leaflets near Wonokromo and Perak, we continued our flight toward Modjokerto and Madioen. Above Solo, we aimed some bundles right into the sultan's kraton. As we neared Semarang, we spotted two Jap fighters on the airstrip at Kali Benteng. We strafed them and saw the Japs scatter.

"Above Ambarawa, we *accidentally discovered* the infamous concentration camps. The women and children ran around excitedly when they saw this strange airplane with its giant red, white and blue flag on the tail, and our leaflets coming down. We looked down on this scene *with great emotion*, and made several passes over this group of camps. The Japanese were apparently too stunned by our appearance to try even one shot at the plane.

"We then flew toward Magelang and via the Boeroeboedoer to Djogja, where we paid special attention to the sultan's palace grounds. While it was tempting to drop more leaflets over Java, our fuel gauges told us it was high time to head for home. We set our course for Broome. In the meantime the weather had worsened and it became difficult to see our entry point on the coast line. Our navigator, de Jongh, was unable to get a radio signal from Broome and our own navigation instruments were thrown off by the weather. We began to run low on fuel when we guessed that we were still fifty miles from Broome. Enormous monsoon clouds made any visual orientation impossible and the engines began to cough. We landed at Broome with only a few drops of gasoline left over."

The above is my translation of an excerpt from **The Forgotten Squadron** *which was mailed out to Mother and Annelies by the Banjoe Biroe reunion committee in Nederland. Annelies Zweede traveled to Nederland and attended the reunion in April 1991.*

Sunset Over Java

   *Jan Roel and Kia de Vries as well as Bert and Connie
de Vries traveled to Nederland in 1997 to attend a reunion
of survivors of the Fifteenth Battalion camp.*

Annotated Bibliography

Because of my life-long interest in Indonesia and the years of combat and turmoil during and after World War Two, I have tried to provide appropriate historical context for this personal memoir. The following books provided a great deal of information and are in my personal library.

Behl, Edward. *Hirohito: Behind the Myth*. (New York: Villard Books, 1989).

Explores the extent of the Emperor's involvement in the war, including his knowledge of the plan to attack Pearl Harbor, his awareness of the atrocities being committed against the Chinese, as well as Japan's grotesquely barbaric bacteriological warfare experiments on thousands of Allied prisoners of war.

Blair, Joan and Clay, Jr. *Return from the River Kwai*. (New York: Simon & Schuster, 1979).

The nightmare story of Allied prisoners of war being put to work on the railroad connecting Thailand and Burma. Upon being shipped to work as slaves in the mines of Japan and Manchuria, a number of their unmarked Japanese "Hell Ships" were torpedoed by the US Navy. A few survived to be rescued by American submarines.

Bradley, James. *Flyboys*. (New York: Little Brown, 2003).

The story of nine American airmen who disappeared after bombing the fortified Pacific island of Chichi Jima, a sister island of Iwo Jima. All were shot down, but one was rescued by an American submarine. His name was George H. W. Bush, who would later become President of the United States. The other eight fighter pilots were captured and executed by the Japanese garrison. The facts about their gruesome deaths were suppressed for years by the Japanese and American governments after the war. After beheading the flyers, Admiral Mori demanded delivery of their livers, to be eaten along with other body parts.

Brooks, Janice Young. *Guests of the Emperor*. (New York: Ballantine Books, 1990).

One of the most readable, true stories of the British and Australian women who fled Singapore by ship, were bombed and swam ashore on Sumatra. This group included Australian Army nurses, of whom 21 were massacred by the Japs as they swam toward the beach. These shipwreck survivors were imprisoned with the Dutch women and children who had lived on Sumatra before the war, including Mrs. van Zanen and her three daughters, Jeannette, Han and Willemien. After the war, Jeannette van Zanen married my step-brother Alexander K. (Bob) Zweede, so she became part of our family. This is the same group whose starvation, neglect and humiliation is documented by Helen Colijn in "Song of Survival" (see below). Made into an NBC documentary.

Buruma, Ian. *The Wages of Guilt: Memories of War in Germany and Japan*. (New York: Farrar Strauss & Giroux, 1994).

Analysis of why it is that the younger generation in Germany has come to terms with what their parents did during the war, while the Japanese have ignored and denied it. At Tokyo's Yasukuni Shrine, displays glorify troops "liberating" East Asia from colonialists and communists. A Shinto priest there told Buruma, "The Asian people are still grateful." At a memorial to kamikaze pilots who died for the Emperor, the museum director says the flyers "sincerely believed in peace."

Chang, Iris. *The Rape of Nanking: The Forgotten Holocaust of World War II.* (New York, Basic Books, 1997).

In December 1937, the Japanese Army swept into the ancient capital of China, and within weeks not only looted and burned the defenseless city but systematically raped, tortured and murdered more than 300,000 Chinese civilians. The story of this atrocity continues to be denied by the Japanese government. Those who would now prefer that I not refer to the aggressors of the Pacific War as Japs because that is no longer "politically correct" should first read this book, as well as Gavan Daws' book *Prisoners of the Japanese*.

Charles, Robert H. *Last Man Out.* (Austin, TX: Eakin Press, 1988).

Charles was a Marine on board the USS *Houston* who fought in the Battle of the Java Sea and survived the sinking of his battleship in the Battle of the Sunda Strait. His group of POWs was put to work on the infamous Siam-Burma railroad, where many were worked to death as slaves. A Dutch Army doctor, Henri Hekking risked his life to save hundreds of American and Australian prisoners, including the author. His knowledge of tropical herbs allowed Doc Hekking to treat the sick and injured men when there were no modern medicines available. An estimated 100,000 Allied prisoners of war died in 14 months to build this railroad for the Japs.

Colijn, Helen. *Song of Survival: Women Interned.* (Ashland: White Cloud Press, 1995).

This true story about the camps on Sumatra was made into the movie "Paradise Road" starring Glenn Close as the *a capella* choir director. My future sister-in-law, Jeannette van Zanen-Zweede, as well as her mother and two sisters were imprisoned in these same camps, with the British missionaries, the society matrons from Singapore and

Australian Army nurses. Jeannette's mother, Annie van Zanen died of starvation; the death rate was one of the highest in all of the civilian prison camps. Mrs. van Zanen is mentioned in the book and Jeannette is thanked in the acknowledgements.

This video is *highly recommended* for anyone interested in forming a mental image of the women's camps and how ordinary people behave under extraordinary conditions.

Cook, Hatuko Taya and Theodore F. *Japan at War: An Oral History*. (New York: The New Press, 1992).

A compelling oral history, collected from the Japanese military and civilians who lived through the war. Chilling insights into the intentional cruelty of the Nipponese Army and their medieval warrior's Bushido code, which regards anyone who surrenders in war as sub-human. Gruesome confessions by Japs who participated in unspeakable atrocities, including the bacteriological warfare experiments on Allied prisoners of war. There was just as much, if not more, racism on the part of the Jap aggressors as there was on the part of the Western military and civilian whites in South East Asia.

Cortesi, Lawrence. *The Battle for Manila.* **(New York: Zebra Books, 1984).**

The Japanese commander decides to defend Manila to the last man, committing some of the worst atrocities of World War II against the Filipino civilians and utterly destroying the city.

Costello, John. *The Pacific War.* **(New York: Rawson Wade Publishers, 1981).**

History of the origins and conduct of World War II in the Pacific, based on hitherto secret archives. A comprehensive and well-illustrated account, with insights from Allied and Japanese participants. Japan's aggression in China eventually required the conquest of the oil fields in the Netherlands East Indies, which in turn required the neutralization of the American Navy at Pearl Harbor, its Army Air Force at Manila and the British Navy at Singapore.

Daws, Gavan. *Prisoners of the Japanese: POWs of World War II in the Pacific.* **(New York: Wm. Morrow, 1994).**

The famous and definitive book about the Allied prisoners of war (British, Australian, American and Dutch). In the eyes of the Japanese, white men who allowed themselves to be captured in war were despicable. They deserved to die. The Japs viewed Caucasians as racially inferior, incomprehensible and indeed barely human. The prisoners instinctively form themselves into small groups with similar backgrounds, forming what Daws calls "tribes." The Dutch prisoners had a higher survival rate because they had been acclimated to the tropics and their Dutch doctors proved especially skilled and devoted in treating tropical wounds and infections. The book includes the infamous Bataan Death March, the nightmare conditions on the Siam-Burma railway, and the senseless cruelty on board Hell Ships transporting weak prisoners to Japan for slave labor in the mines. Newly translated into the Dutch language.

de Vries, Dirk. *Gordel van Smaragd: Land en Volk van Indonesië*. (Amsterdam: Uitgeverij Contact, 1946).

A beautiful book of 180 photos showing what Nederlands Indië looked like before the war. The title (which translates as Emerald Belt), refers to the islands draped around the equator.

de Vries, Jacobus E. *War Came to Java* (private printing, Morristown, NJ, 1998).

Referred to in the text above; 245 pages. The edited oral history of Professor Bert de Vries and Lexie Zweede, covering their early years in Nederland and their very different lives on Java before and during World War II. Describes the Zweede and de Vries families during these turbulent years. Contains postscripts by my brothers and sisters, as well as numerous family photos, maps and an extensive epilogue.

Groen, P.M.H. *Mededelingen van de Sectie Militaire Geschiedenis Landmachtstaf's Gravenhage*, **deel 8, 1985).**

The official Army history of the hostage crisis in and around the concentration camps of Banjoe Biroe and Ambarawa. Excellent, first person accounts of the fire-fights and negotiations required to evacuate the Dutch civilian prisoners from central Java after the Japanese capitulation in September 1945. Describes the attack on the hospital in Magelang (where Mrs. Zweede, Annelies and Johan were being treated) by the Indonesian terrorists, as well as the hair-breadth escape to Semarang under protection of a handful of Gurkha troops and British officers. Touches on the conflicting military, economic and diplomatic interests of Britain, the Netherlands and the newly-declared Republic of Indonesia.

Hartley, M. G. *Mijn Kamp: Niet door Hitler.* **(Amsterdam: Amsterdamse Boek en Courantmaatschappij, 1947).**

Drawings and text about life in the camps at Tjimahi, near Bandoeng, West Java. A marvelous collection of 120 drawings and bitterly humorous text, made by Hartley and hidden from the guards. The three Tjimahi camps contained about 10,000 male civilian and military prisoners, among them Bob Zweede and my Uncle Lo Berg.

Hillen, Ernest. *The Way of a Boy: A Memoir of Java.* (New York: Penguin Books, 1994).

The account of a Dutch family living on a tea plantation in West Java before the war and their imprisonment by the Japanese. Ernest was a young boy of about ten. His mother and brother wound up in the same "Bloemenkamp" in Bandoeng that the de Vries family was in, before the Hillens were moved across the road to the much larger "Tjihapit" camp for civilian women and children. The entire Hillen family survived the camps and moved to Canada.

Hillenbrand, Laura. *Unbroken*. (New York, Random House, 2010).

The unforgettable story of Louie Zamperini, the American athlete and airman who crashed in the Pacific, and endured thirst and hunger for endless days and nights in an open raft. Captured by the Japanese, he was beaten and tortured for months. This best-seller has been made into a major movie by the same title. This is a powerful testament to the sadism of the Jap guards, Zamperini's incredible will power, and the resilience of the human mind, body and spirit.

Hornfischer, James L. *Ship of Ghosts*. New York: Bantam Books, 2006).

This is the story of the USS *Houston* and her sinking during the battle of the Sunda Strait in February 1942. The survivors were brought ashore and jailed in Pandeglang, where the three youngest de Vries children saw some of them. The dwindling number of Navy survivors were forced to work on the infamous Burma-Thailand Death Railway. The title of the book refers to the fact that the USS *Houston* had been reported as sunk by the Japanese several times, at different locations. As a result, the fate of the *Houston* remained a mystery until the end of the war. She was referred to as the "Galloping Ghost of the Java Coast." The ship's crew numbered 1,168 as she entered battle. Just 291 returned home.

Keith, Agnes Newton. *Three Came Home*. (Boston, Little Brown, 1947).

One of the earliest books about the British civilian prisoners on Borneo. A true classic.

Keizer-Heuzeveldt. *En de Lach Keerde Terug*. (Franeker: Uitgeverij Wever, 1982).

An excellent short book about the Indonesian Revolution against the return of the Dutch Government, and the hair-raising experiences of this newly-freed family in the

Semarang region of central Java. The title may be loosely translated as "We did recover our sense of humor."

Kennedy, Paul. *Pacific Onslaught.* (New York: Ballantine Books, 1972).

This is a concise and well-illustrated history of Japan's aggression during the first two years following its attack on Pearl Harbor. After its easy victories in early 1942 and the conquest of the Netherlands East Indies, the Japanese Navy's "victory disease" was so strong that it proposed the invasion of Australia itself, but this was firmly rejected by the Army which still had its attention riveted upon completing its conquest of China. Instead, they agreed to limited campaigns in Burma and the South Pacific to cut the Allied supply lines to China and Australia.

Kennedy, Paul. *The Rise and Fall of the Great Powers: Economic Change and Military Conflict from 1500 to 2000.* (New York: Ballantine Books, 1987).

In this best-seller, Kennedy presents a wide-ranging analysis of global power politics over the past five centuries. This British-born Yale historian focuses on the critical relationship of economic power and military strength as it affects the rise and fall of empires – from imperial Spain to the British Empire and the new Pax Americana.

Kousbroek, Rudy. *Het Oostindisch Kampsyndroom.*
(Amsterdam, Meulenhoff, 1992).

This is a collection of articles written by Kousbroek and
others, concerning the daily life in the Netherlands East
Indies, before and during the war. Also included are a
number of essays about the adjustment to life in Nederland
after the war, for both Dutch and Indonesians evacuated
from the Indies. This is an intense reappraisal of the
complex bond that grew between the Dutch, the
Indonesians, and the tropical islands where they both grew
up. Kousbroek lived on Sumatra before the war and was
imprisoned there as a boy.

Leffelaar, H. L. *De Japanse Regering Betaalt Aan
Toonder.* **(Alphen aan de Rijn: Sijthoff, 1980).**

A well-illustrated book about a Dutch family living on
Sumatra and their imprisonment in a number of different
camps, culminating in Kamp Si Rengo-Rengo, in northern
Sumatra.

Lord, Walter. *Lonely Vigil: Coastwatchers of the
Solomons.* **(New York: Viking Press, 1977).**

In Admiral Halsey's words: "The coastwatchers saved
Guadalcanal and Guadalcanal saved the Pacific." The story
of the natives who risked their lives as coastwatchers in the
Solomon Islands and made a major contribution to the

critically important battles on Guadalcanal and in the waters of Ironbottom Sound.

MacGillavry, Annemie. *Je Kunt Niet Altijd Huilen.* (Bussum: De Kern, 1978).

Subtitled: The broken lives of a Dutch family during the war years in the Indies. One of the best Dutch books about life in the Indies before the war and what it was like to be in the Japanese prison camps. The title can be roughly translated as, "You cannot cry all the time."

McCabe Elliott, Inger. *Batik—Fabled Cloth of Java.* (New York: Clarkson N. Potter, 1984).

This is a lavishly illustrated book describing the historical roots of batik clothing, where and how it was made in the past and how this art form is once again flourishing, especially on Java and Bali. The author provides some fascinating history, such as the fact that Sir Thomas Stamford Raffles was the first Westerner to chronicle a systematic study of batik in his famous book *History of Java*. Raffles ruled Java on behalf of Britain after Holland had been conquered by Napoleon in the early 1800s.

McKew Parr, Charles. *The Voyages of David de Vries.* **(New York: Thomas Y. Crowell Co., 1969).**

Born in Hoorn in 1593, this famous sea captain served as the right hand man to Governor General Coen in the Dutch East India Company at the fortified town of Batavia. The dangerous voyages to the Indies, via the Cape of Good Hope, usually took seven months. He subsequently sailed to the Americas in 1632, where he attempted to establish a *patroonate* on the Delaware River at Zwaanendael, the present Lewes, Delaware. David Pietersz de Vries also sailed the Mediterranean and the Caribbean as a private merchant skipper and privateer. He explored what is now the eastern seaboard of the United States, visiting the English at Jamestown, the Swedes at the present site of Philadelphia, sailing up the Hudson River and undertaking a diplomatic mission to the English colony at Hartford on behalf of the Dutch government at Fort Amsterdam, now Manhattan.

Manchester, William. *American Caesar: Douglas MacArthur 1880 - 1964.* **(New York: Dell, 1978).**

The best-selling biography of General MacArthur. Chronicles his vanity and his incredible blunders at the outset of the war, as well as his subsequent triumphs, as his forces leap-frogged from Australia to New Guinea and the Philippines. The day after Pearl Harbor was attacked, ignoring many warnings, MacArthur allowed all of his aircraft to be destroyed on the ground at Clark Field near Manila by the Japanese Air Force.

Manchester, William. *Goodbye Darkness: A Memoir of the Pacific*. **(Boston: Little Brown, 1979).**
Manchester returns to visit the battlefields where he fought as a young Marine: Guadalcanal, Saipan and Okinawa.

Miles, Milton E. *A Different Kind of War: The Unknown Story of the U.S. Navy's Guerrilla Forces in World War II China*. **(Garden City, NY: Doubleday, 1967).**

In spite of overwhelmingly difficult conditions, Admiral Miles established a network of Chinese and American guerrilla fighters along the Japanese-occupied Chinese coast in order to prepare for an American invasion and also to report the weather conditions that were of vital importance to the US Navy fighting in the South China Sea. Admiral and Mrs. Miles became good friends of our family during the 1950s in Washington.

Miles, Giles. *Nathaniel's Nutmeg*. **(New York, Penguin Books, 1999).**

An exciting account of the dangerous voyages, bizarre transactions, and desperate battles of the spice wars. At the beginning of the seventeenth century, the tiny island of Run, in a remote region of Indonesia became the focal point of maritime wars between Portugal, Holland and England. Run's harvest of nutmeg turned it into the most lucrative of the Spice Islands because nutmeg was said to combat the bubonic plague. The outcome of the fighting was one of the most spectacular deals in history: Britain ceded Run to Holland but in return was given Manhattan.

Netherlands Institute for War Documentation.
Representing the Japanese Occupation of Indonesia.
(Waanders Publishers, Zwolle, 1999).

A well-illustrated book that offers a survey of the way in which Indonesia, Japan and the Netherlands have shaped the memory of the war years. This major work also includes commentary about the various radio and TV programs produced in Holland in later years, dealing with the Japanese occupation.

Pakenham, Thomas. *The Boer War.* (New York: Random House, 1979).

This detailed and lavishly-illustrated account is considered the standard text on the subject. When Britain attacked in October of 1899, the public expected the campaign to be over by Christmas, but the Boer War proved to be the longest (33 months), costliest, bloodiest and most humiliating war the British had fought between 1815 and 1914. When the Boer women continued to shelter and supply their men in prolonged guerilla campaigns, Lord Kitchener herded them together in "concentration camps." His neglect of elementary sanitation led to epidemics of typhoid and dysentery. At least 20,000 died in history's first civilian concentration camps, mostly women and children.

Parkin, Ray. *Out of the Smoke*. (New York: Wm. Morrow Press, 1960).

The first-hand account of the sinking of the Australian cruiser *Perth* in the Battle of the Sunda Strait in March of 1942, days after the disastrous Battle of the Java Sea. While most of the Australian survivors were captured and imprisoned by the Japs, ten sailors attempt an open-ocean escape to Australia in a life boat, among them Ray Parkin. His second book about his POW years in Burma is called *Into the Smother*.

Prange, Gordon W. *At Dawn We Slept*. (New York: McGraw Hill, 1981).

The definitive book about Japan's sneak attack on the American fleet at Pearl Harbor, and all the circumstances surrounding the disaster.

Prange, Gordon W. *Miracle at Midway*. (New York: McGraw Hill, 1982).

Chronicles how desperately obsolete our torpedo bombers were and how few carriers the US Navy had at this critical turning point in the war.

Schenk, M.G and J. B. Spaan. *Paleis Noordeinde en Zijn Bewoners.* **(Baarn: De Boekerij, NV).**

A beautifully illustrated booklet about the royal palace in downtown Den Haag. Traces the earliest beginnings of this palace compound, begun in 1591 and lived in by each of Nederland's kings and queens. After the fire in 1948 the palace is largely abandoned until Queen Juliana and the Government agreed to make it available to the envisioned Institute of Social Studies. The Government's restoration was begun in 1961 and completed in 1966.

Sides, Hampton. *Ghost Soldiers.* **New York: Random House, 2001).**

Because the Japanese had begun executing American POW's in Palawan, in the Philippines, it was feared that the prisoners at the Cabanatuan prison camp would be massacred as the US Army approached to liberate them. In June of 1945, 121 hand-selected Army Rangers, aided by Filipino guerillas moved 30 miles to rescue the 513 American survivors of this hellish prison camp. This is a dazzling account of one of the greatest rescue missions in history.

Stichting Jongens in Japanse Kampen 1942-1945, *Wij Weten van Hoe*. Hans Liesker, ed. (Gouda, NL, Electronic Printcenter, 2005).

A collection of stories and diaries about the boy's camps in Ambarawa. The title can be loosely translated as "We Know All About It." The purpose of this relatively recent book is to explore the emotional crosscurrents experienced by the boys in Kamp 7 during the war, as well as their adjustments in later years in Nederland. Questions raised by the grandchildren of camp survivors are also explored in light of our current perspective and understanding.

Toland, John. *The Rising Sun: The Decline and Fall of the Japanese Empire.* (New York: Bantam Books, 1970).

The historical account of the forces leading to Japan's invasion of Korea, Manchuria and China in the 1930's, which in turn led to its confrontation with Britain, the United States, the Netherlands East Indies and Australia. Within a few days of launching its expanded war southward, the Japs knocked out the three pillars of the overconfident Allied defense of South East Asia: the American battle fleet at Hawaii, the American Army Air Force at Clark Field in the Philippines and the British Navy as it tried to halt the invasion of Malaya.

van der Post, Laurens. *The Admiral's Baby.* **(New York: Wm. Morrow, 1996).**

This British Army officer was captured on Java and imprisoned in Batavia and Bandoeng, West Java, where he met Ray Parkin, one of the Australian Navy survivors of the Battle of the Sunda Strait. (See Parkin's *Out of the Smoke*). When the end of the war was announced, Colonel van der Post was the first ex-POW to meet with Admiral Patterson on the British cruiser Cumberland when it arrived off Batavia to take the surrender of the Japanese commander of Java on September 30, 1945. This book is a most revealing account of the extremely difficult position of the British military when they were suddenly called upon to disarm the Japanese and rescue the military and civilian prisoners in the Netherlands East Indies.
The atomic bombs shortened the war, leaving the American and British troops as yet far away from the Indies.

Upon their arrival they found that Indonesian nationalism had taken root during the Japanese occupation. But the Dutch Government in Europe was completely ignorant of the true state of affairs in Asia and insisted that Dutch rule be re-instated, by force of arms if necessary. For the thankless task of trying to disarm the Nipponese and rescue the newly-freed prisoners, the British lost 600 lives while 1400 were wounded in their battles with the Indonesian terrorists.

van der Post, Laurens. *The Prisoner and the Bomb*. (New York: Wm. Morrow Press, 1970).

This famous South African author was a British Colonel, who fought on in the wilds of Bantam province in West Java after the Allied surrender. He was captured and imprisoned by the Japs in Bandoeng. Were it not for the atomic bombs dropped on Japan, millions more would have died on both sides of the conflict, and especially the Allied prisoners. After the war, General Terauchi's orders were found in Saigon, directing the massacre of all Allied POW's and civilians, as the Allies neared their camps.

van der Vat, Dan. *The Pacific Campaign: The US-Japanese Naval War: 1941-1945*. (New York: Simon & Schuster, 1991).

A meticulously researched and definitive account of the US-Japanese naval actions, with good maps and photos. Provides details about the Battles of the Java Sea and Sunda Strait, as well as Balikpapan, from the enemy archives and eye-witness accounts as well.

van Heekeren, Cees. *Trekkers en Blijvers*. (Franeker: T. Wever, 1980).

A most delightful book about a Dutch family from Den Haag that is drawn to the Indies over the span of several generations. Cees van Heekeren and his wife arrived in Indië in 1938 and lived in the same area of Northern

Sumatra where the van Zanen family lived. They too were imprisoned on Sumatra, survived and returned to Holland, only to be drawn back to the Indonesia they loved. They experienced the continued fighting between the Dutch and Indonesian terrorists in Batavia and even attempted to work for a Dutch bank operating under the new Indonesian regime.

van Mook, Dr. H. J. *Indonesië, Nederland en de Wereld.* (Amsterdam: De Bezige Bij, 1949).

This book by Dr. van Mook, who became Acting Governor General of the Netherlands East Indies after the Japanese surrendered, sheds light on the impossible situation of the Provisional NEI Government in dealing with the Dutch Government in The Hague, the British military and the Indonesian nationalists. Every time van Mook painstakingly negotiated a tentative agreement with the Indonesians, his uninformed and rigid superiors in Holland overruled him. Peace negotiations were held with the Indonesians, but agreements were soon broken. Undisciplined gangs continued to attack the British and Dutch military in spite of cease-fire agreements. The United Nations forced Holland to abandon the military operations aimed at enforcing the agreements negotiated with the Indonesians. Australia and the USA were particularly opposed to the return of the Netherlands East Indies Government.

van Velden, Dr. Dora. *De Japanse_Burgerkampen*. (Franeker: Uitgeverij T. Wever, 1976).

This is the definitive book (at 620 pages) about the Japanese civilian concentration camps during World War II; it has an English summary. The book describes the camps in the Netherlands East Indies as well as those in Malaya, the Philippines, Burma, Thailand, Japan, Formosa and Manchuria. The author herself was imprisoned in Tjideng, on Java.

Dr. van Velden summarizes the number of prisoners in each of the camps, and where such information is available, the number of prisoners who died in each location. The camps on Sumatra where the van Zanens were interned are described as having some of the highest death rates, up to 38%. The death rates in the Japanese jails, such as Tjipinang, where my father was, reached 60 to 70%. The author also mentions the Dutch Government's proclamation that all civilians should continue in their jobs as long as the Japs allowed, in order to keep essential public services going (the "Nippon werkers").

This book also contains a wealth of photographs taken by the first Red Cross and RAPWI teams to reach the camps in 1945. A significant number of these photos were taken in Banjoe Biroe Kamp 10 in central Java, where Lex Zweede, with Annelies and Johan, as well as Joan and I, were waiting for the British troops.

Winchester, Simon. *Krakatoa*. (New York, HarperCollins, 2003).

The story of the annihilation in 1883 of the volcano-island of Krakatoa, in the Sunda Strait. This catastrophic eruption created an immense tsunami that killed nearly forty thousand people on Java and Sumatra. Dust swirled around the planet for years, causing temperatures to drop around the world. The most western portion of Java was inundated and blasted by the superheated dust cloud. Even in 1941, when my family visited the Sunda Strait and Pandeglang, this region was still sparsely inhabited.

Winslow, Commander Walter G., USN. *The Ghost of the Java Coast*. Satellite Beach: Coral Reef, 1974).

Winslow fought the Jap Navy on board the American battleship USS *Houston* during the battles of the Java Sea and Sunda Strait. According to Ray Parkin's account in *Out of the Smoke*, all of the wounded seamen of HMAS *Perth* and most of the other survivors of that ship and the *Houston* surrendered to the Japanese at Labuan on the shores of the Sunda Strait separating Java and Sumatra. They were moved inland to the town of Menes and then to Serang, Batavia and eventually to Burma. The only road leading inland from Labuan goes through the little hamlet of Pandeglang where Juffie, Bert, Joan and I were staying at that time.

Yergin, Daniel. *The Prize: The Epic Quest for Oil, Money and Power.* **(New York: Simon & Schuster, 1991).**

This Pulitzer Prize-winning book begins with the discovery of oil in Pennsylvania, the Rockefellers, Royal Dutch Shell, Russian Oil and the Iranian Oil Company. Describes the critical role played by the American oil fields during World War I and especially during World War II. Explains Japan's urgent need for oil and the other resources of the Netherlands East Indies if it is to continue its conquest of China. Oil was the Prize. Made into a PBS television series.

Made in the USA
Columbia, SC
29 July 2023

20933814R00124